Graham Lock was born in Sidmouth, Devon in 1948 and has been a keen music fan since the early 1960s. He writes regularly about jazz for *Gramophone* and also reviews classical recordings for the *BBC Music Magazine*. From 1987 to 1991 he was Deputy Editor of *The Wire*. His work has appeared in numerous publications, including *Jazz – The Magazine, New Musical Express, Opera Now, Jazzthetik, Let It Rock* and *City Limits*. He is a contributor to *The Good Jazz Guide, Contemporary Composers* and *The Guinness Who's Who Of Jazz*. He has also written programme notes for the Arts Council's Contemporary Music Network tours and cd-insert notes for several record labels. He is currently researching aspects of jazz history at Nottingham University and continues to work as a freelance journalist.

His previous book, *Forces In Motion: Anthony Braxton And The Metareality Of Creative Music*, received the highest critical acclaim:

"A sympathetic and penetrating study— it's a compelling read."
The Guardian

"A brilliant performance— Other reviews have lauded this book as one of the best jazz studies ever. That's about right, too."
NME

"A fascinating and indispensable introduction to a music of real and immediate importance."
The Times Literary Supplement

"One of the few books that tries to move inside the music itself— It is absolutely essential reading."
The Wire

"One of the best biographies of a jazz musician I have yet seen."
Time Out

"One of the best books on a master musician's art and life I've read."
Cadence

Chasing The Vibration

– A Stride Conversation Piece –

CHASING THE VIBRATION

Meetings With Creative Musicians

GRAHAM LOCK

with photographs by
Nick White

CHASING THE VIBRATION
First edition 1994
© 1994 Graham Lock
except 'Invisible At All Times'
and 'Waltzing With Fire'
© *New Musical Express* 1983.
All rights reserved

ISBN 1 873012 81 0 *(paperback)*
ISBN 1 873012 82 9 *(hardback)*

Photographs © 1994 Nick White

Cover design Joe Pieczenko

A Stride Conversation Piece
published by
Stride Publications
11 Sylvan Road, Exeter
Devon EX4 6EW

To Sun Ra, June Tyson, John Gilmore and the Arkestra
– thank you for the beauty and the magic

Contents

Acknowledgements *11*
Introduction: *Chasing The Vibration* *13*

Steve Lacy *The Tao Of Soprano* *17*
Cecil Taylor *Invisible At All Times* *23*
Mal Waldron *Waltzing With Fire* *35*
Abdullah Ibrahim *In Struggle, In Grace* *44*
Chris McGregor *An African Way Of Swing* *57*
Billie Holiday *The Lady And The Legend* (review) *64*
Mike Westbrook *Sweet Thunder* *67*
Norma Winstone *The Singing Is The Song* *77*
Max Roach *Cymbals Of Change* *82*
Betty Carter *In Her Own Sweet Way* *89*
Horace Tapscott *The Tapscott Sessions* (review) *96*
The Guest Stars *Ironing In The Soul* *99*
Marilyn Crispell *At The Square Root Of Energy* *105*
Dave Holland *In Pursuit Of The Cubist Bass Line* *112*
Sunny Murray *Is It A Bus? Is It A Tiger?* *119*
Jimmy Giuffre *Coming In From The Cool* *127*
Kenny Wheeler *The Trumpet Shall Sound* *135*
Leo Smith *Procession Of The Great Ancestry* (review) *142*
Sun Ra *The Mysteries Of Mr Ra* *144*
John Gilmore *Big John's Special* *156*
Evan Parker *Speaking Of The Essence* *164*

Discographical Update *181*

Acknowledgements

I owe an immense debt of gratitude to all the musicians who have taken the time to discuss their work with me in the last 15 years. In addition to the artists featured in this book, they include Robyn Archer, Billy Bang, Tim Berne, Arthur Blythe, Lester Bowie, Deirdre Cartwright, Vladimir Chekasin, Ornette Coleman, Nathan Davis, Jack DeJohnette, Mark Dresser, Jim Dvorak, Vyacheslav Ganelin, Vinny Golia, Barry Guy, Charlie Haden, Gerry Hemingway, Earl Hines, Ken Hyder, Jan Kopinski, Malachi Favors Maghostut, Tania Maria, Bobby McFerrin, Phil Minton, Roscoe Mitchell, Maggie Nicols, Sam Rivers, Hal Russell, Irene Schweizer, Archie Shepp, Wadada Leo Smith, John Surman, Vladimir Tarasov, Henry Threadgill, Julie Tippetts, Randy Weston, Annie Whitehead and John Zorn. A special 'thank you' is due to the various members of the Sun Ra Arkestra who were kind enough to answer my questions during our trip to Liverpool: Ahmed Abdullah, Marshall Allen, Tyrone Hill, John Ore, Noel Scott and the very gracious June Tyson.

    I am, of course, grateful to the people who, over the years, have commissioned the articles, interviews, insert-notes etc that fuelled my interest in the music. They are (in approximately chronological order) Neil Spencer at *NME*, Penny Valentine and David Ilic at *City Limits*, Anthony Wood and Richard Cook at *The Wire*, Isabel Appio at *Black Beat International*, Werner X. Uehlinger at hat ART Records, Leo Feigin at Leo Records, Fred Maroth at Music & Arts, Madelyn Cohen, Rachel Sinfield and Dorothy Wright at the CMN, Tony Russell at *Jazz – The Magazine*, Colin Larkin at Square One Books, Steve Lake at ECM Records, Keith Shadwick at *Gramophone* and Christine Stephan at

Jazzthetik. A lot of people in the music business have been extremely helpful in facilitating interviews, providing information and recordings etc, so many thanks to Ken Ansell and Paul Acott-Stevens at Impetus, Donald Clarke at Chief, Jo Nagle and Jo Pratt at Blue Note, Caroll Pinkham at Serious/Speakout, Karen Pitchford at Koch International, Stephen Sanderson at New Note, Paul Smith at Blast First and, definitely not least, Laurie Staff and Ron Warshaw at Harmonia Mundi.

I am particularly pleased to have the chance to record my appreciation for the support that a number of friends and colleagues have provided over the years. These are the people whose warmth and encouragement have helped to keep body and soul together. They include Anthony Braxton, Marilyn Charlton, Teri Connolly, Marilyn Crispell, Nicole Dalle, Peter and Freda Davis, Jan Diakow, Dave Downing, Jeff Eaman, John Fordham, Malcolm Green, Andy Hamilton, Andy Isham, Barry and Christina Jones, Nick Kimberley, Phil and Cath McNeill, Ron Mendel, Stephen C. Middleton, Chrissie Murray, Chris Parker, Brian Priestley, Susie Roth, Victor Schonfield, Annie Street, Roger Thomas, Lucy Ward, Lucy Whitman, Val Wilmer, Nigel Wright and Katy Zeserson. I am especially indebted to Nick White, who has been a close friend and colleague for many years. He has attended innumerable interviews and concerts with me and has always produced fantastic photographs, even in the most trying of circumstances. I am delighted that Nick agreed to my including several of his photographs in this book. (The cover photo of Sun Ra, incidentally, comes from what I think was our first assignment together, back in 1983.)

I am very glad that Rupert Loydell of Stride Publications suggested this book to me, and I appreciate his patience with my tardiness and prevarications. It is a refreshing change to meet a publisher who knows and loves the music. Thanks too to the current *NME* editor Steve Sutherland for permission to reprint the Cecil Taylor and Mal Waldron pieces, on which *NME* retain the copyright; and to Hackney Council for their upkeep of Clissold Park, a favourite spot that has often helped to keep the blues at bay.

Finally, my heartfelt thanks as always to my parents, George and Una Taylor, for their continuing love and support.

Graham Lock
October 1993

INTRODUCTION
Chasing The Vibration

Mysteries, mysteries. Why jazz? Why me? How did I, growing up white and middle-class in a sleepy Devon seaside town, end up here, writing this? I'm not even sure how or when it began. With the Beatles, who made the first music I loved? With Mal Waldron and Eric Dolphy, whose *The Quest* was the first jazz record to turn my head? Yet I heard that lp in 1967 and it was another ten years before I began to explore jazz in depth, five more again before I began to write about it regularly.

Another starting-point was *Let It Rock*, the first music magazine I wrote for. That was in the mid-70s. In 1978 I moved to London and began working for *NME*. I wrote mostly about pop at first, but my love of jazz had been growing steadily: already I was a fan of Clifford Brown, John Coltrane, Andrew Hill, Billie Holiday, Thelonious Monk, Lester Young. I remember too some wonderful concerts from the late 70s/early 80s: the Art Ensemble Of Chicago at the Roundhouse; Ornette Coleman and Abdullah Ibrahim at different Bracknell Festivals; Art Pepper at St Paul's Church, Hammersmith. Sun Ra at the Venue was something else again – was it then the magic took root in my soul?

My first interview with a jazz musician took place in 1979; a brief, backstage encounter with Earl Hines. For various reasons, that turned out pretty much a farce, and I was further discouraged when *NME* waited nearly a year to run the piece. But in 1982 I gave it a second shot, and luckily my next interviewee was Steve Lacy, who proved both friendly and forthcoming. Meetings with Archie Shepp, Cecil Taylor and Mal Waldron followed in quick succession. A little later, the previously quarterly *Wire* magazine went monthly, offering a regular outlet for interviews with jazz musicians. I began to form the notion that here was a path I could follow. This book documents several of my encounters along that path in the ensuing years. (I wish there had been room to include more: however, the meeting that really sealed my fate – with Anthony Braxton – I've already written about in my book *Forces In Motion*.)

I had better make clear right away that this is a book of journalism, not a book of criticism or musical analysis. These are nearly all profile pieces, written as introductions to the musicians in question and generally sparked by my curiosity to learn more about the people whose music could so move me. Many were originally written for *The Wire*, although the interviews with Steve Lacy, Cecil Taylor, Mal Waldron and Max Roach first appeared in *NME* and the Sunny Murray piece is previously unpublished. Apart from minor cuts and alterations (plus a few new headings), most of the articles appear here as first published, the main exceptions being that the second part of the Abdullah Ibrahim interview has been shortened, while the Norma Winstone, Sun Ra and Evan Parker pieces have been slightly expanded. I have also added, at the end of each article, the month and year in which the interview took place.

Whatever value such pieces retain is, I think, to be found in what the musicians themselves have to say about their lives and their art. Theirs are the insights that matter. My growing commitment to this belief explains why there is an increasing use of direct quotation and the simple question/answer format in the latter stages of the book, and why, too, I decided to include only a very small number of reviews. I hope, however, that the book also has a degree of documentary value in the glimpses it offers of these artists, many of them giants of 20th century culture. Certainly I feel my life has been enriched by my contacts with these musicians. To have talked with Betty Carter, John Gilmore, Max Roach – these are privileges indeed.

Ralph Ellison once wrote "And yet, who knows very much of what jazz is really about? Or how shall we ever know until we are willing to confront anything and everything which it sweeps across our path?" That "anything and everything" sounds to me like a lifetime's work, and then some. So I'm still chasing the vibration, still wondering how and why this music can touch me so profoundly. I no longer expect to find any definitive answers; but I have learned that when the music calls, you ignore it at your peril. "Beauty," as Sun Ra told me, "is necessary for survival." (Are you listening, Planet Earth?)

The African-American creative music tradition has given us some of the most beautiful sounds of the age. It is a music that nurtures, inspires and renews the spirit. Yet, because of certain historical and cultural prejudices – in which racism and the prevailing capitalist mind-set have played their parts – the music is often neglected, belittled, misunderstood. It would require a very different book to explicate these issues thoroughly, but I believe the disrespect accorded jazz is one of the great intellectual crimes of the century. The hope must be that one day the musicians will be given the honour and gratitude that is their due (and, not least, decent financial recompense); that, in Albert Ayler's gentle phrase, "one day everything will be as it should be". In the meantime, I'd like to think that this book will be received as a small token of thanks for the many happy hours I've spent as a guest in the house of jazz.

October 1993

STEVE LACY
The Tao Of Soprano

MISTERIOSO

It's ten months since Thelonious Monk, the great bebop pianist, died in New York.

On a wet November morning, in a tiny L-shaped hotel room on Haverstock Hill, Steve Lacy, a man who devoted a dozen years to studying Monk tunes, recalls his late friend.

"I played with him for a whole summer once, the summer of 1960. My, that was a long time ago," he murmurs, "22 years ago."

I ask about Monk's reputation as a prickly, enigmatic character.

"Well, I didn't see it. To me, he was beautiful and brilliant. Yeah, he had an enigmatic side. Monk was mysterious. He was his own person. He treated everybody the same and this got him into a lot of trouble.

"He went through hard times, a lot of hostility and miscomprehension, and he had to swallow that. It was amazing he was as cool as he was."

In the last ten years, Monk practically gave up playing live, and became very reclusive.

Lacy nods. "He folded up, yeah. He folded up and wound down. It was like a long, slow decline." He sighs softly. "He was maltreated by promoters, and exploited, and finally he'd had enough, that's my opinion. I went to visit him the year before he died, but I hadn't seen him in years before that 'cause he lived in New York and I lived in Europe, so— I lost him.

"I feel bad about that, too 'cause I think he needed friends toward the end and, well, I was one of 'em, but I was in Europe, there was nothing I could do about that."

Lacy gives a slight shrug;his quiet New York twang has dropped to a whisper. A ghost is in the air.

From 1962-1965, Lacy played only Monk tunes. He wanted, he says, "to find out why they were so beautiful". That dramatic immersion was the last phase of Lacy's own 15-year apprenticeship. After Monk, he found his own music.

THE BEELINE

Lacy, a short wiry man in his late 40s, is now a seminal figure in modern music. The most adventurous soprano player in jazz history, his career has touched nearly all the bases, from Dixieland to avant-garde. Along the way, he inspired Coltrane to take up soprano, has dabbled in electronics, and is currently working with both ballet dancers and Beat poet Brion Gysin.

His non-musical influences are equally diverse: the Chinese philosophical book *Tao Te Ching* was the basis for his masterpiece 'The Way', while the notebooks of Cubist painter Georges Braque form the text for his recent *Tips* lp.

Despite such formidable erudition, and though he can blow as fierce and free as a gale, Lacy's music remains completely accessible. Bright, witty and deft, it draws on both the poignancy of the blues and the bracing rigour of freeform. Whether playing solo or within the confines of his latest sextet, there are few sounds as distinctive or as lovely as Lacy's soprano, with its comet-trails of bare-boned lyricism.

He began, though, on piano. Born in New York City in 1934 to a family of Jewish Russian emigres, the young Lacy gave up piano lessons after he saw Art Tatum play – "I could never have played like that" – and, a little later, inspired by the great New Orleans saxist Sidney Bechet, he took up the soprano.

The early 50s found Lacy in Dixieland bands until, in a remarkable leap, he joined avant-garde pianist Cecil Taylor, then struggling to make his name.

"Cecil was a magnetic personality," Lacy enthuses. "He was so brilliant, so advanced. He knew all the stuff I wanted to know about so

I just followed him around like a bee after the honey."

Taylor's new, complex music met with great hostility from the white jazz establishment. Just to play, he had to endure rip-offs and racist abuse from every petty-minded club owner in town. Those years, says Lacy, were the beginning of his political awareness.

"It was murderous at times. With Cecil, we went through some terrifying stuff – black and white, employers and employees, bad treatment, injustices. That's where my political education began, at Cecil's feet. And now, many years later, I can't forget that, the stuff I saw Cecil go through, and Monk, those things stay with you for the rest of your life. Those are the values."

Lacy stayed with Taylor till the end of the 50s, then went on to play with Gil Evans, Monk and trumpeter Don Cherry, then a member of Ornette Coleman's pioneering free jazz quartet. Later, after those four years working on Monk tunes, Lacy turned back to freeform, touring Europe and South America with African jazzmen Louis Moholo and Johnny Dyani. Finally he settled in Paris and began to assemble the core of his current group: saxist Steve Potts, drummer Oliver Johnson, his wife Irene Aebi on voice, cello and violin.

By the mid-60s he had also started work on his first major composition. Lacy had found 'The Way'.

THE THROES

The story begins back in the late 50s, with Lacy leafing through a friend's discarded book collection. Witter Bynner's translation of the *Tao Te Ching* caught his eye.

"It had nice pictures and it was *thin*," he recounts drily, "and when I tried to read it, the prose was so clear and succinct. It's 2000 years old but it seemed so wise and down to earth. I thought, goddam, nothing has changed! For me, it's like an ethical guide on how to be."

Lacy "chewed over" the *Tao* for years, meanwhile consigning all his attempts at composition to the wastepaper basket. Finally, in 1966, working on a text from the *Tao*, he clicked.

"It always remains Opus One for me. The piece called 'The Way' was the first thing I wrote that we still play. The way I found the way was through 'The Way'."

Like most of Lacy's work, 'The Way' – now a six-part *magnum opus* – blends written and improvised music in a manner which should, he says, "make sense", with no discernible break between the two modes. It is also much-changed over the years: Lacy likes to try out pieces in a variety of contexts then, after a brief time in their "mature" stage, they are "rested" from the repertoire for some years before the reworking process begins anew.

Not surprisingly, Lacy prefers recent lps like *Tips*, *Songs* and *Ballets* to the bulk of his earlier work, though exceptions include *The Gap*, *The Forest And The Zoo* and *The Woe*, which he still regards as a major piece.

The Woe is a harrowing protest at the Vietnam war, a desperate cacophony that incorporates tapes of machine-gun fire and other war noises. It appears to be in stark contrast to the abstract concerns of 'The Way', yet both share a common root. One of Lacy's first protest pieces, 'Chinese Food', performed with Irene Aebi and Richard Teitelbaum in 1966, was based on texts from the *Tao*.

The Woe came later, in the early 70s, when Lacy was living in Paris. His sleevenotes report that it was "almost unbearable to perform and we were all greatly relieved when it became no longer necessary to do it". What had he meant by *necessary*?

"A matter of life and death, of trying to stay alive in the face of an approaching death. What happened with *The Woe* was, we couldn't ignore the war, we were *in* the war, therefore to stay in the music we had to let the war in the music, and the music became war.

"When you couldn't even play without thinking about that political stuff, what's the solution? To stop playing? No, it's to let the politics right in the music. We chose to let the war in and to fight for our lives. I think if we hadn't done that, it would have killed us, at least temporarily. Killed the spirit. You can't go on with your normal art if the world is falling around your shoulders."

But does such political art have any impact out there in the world?

"Do you think Picasso's *Guernica* had any effect? Maybe not right away, but it certainly weighs something. And Goya's *The Disasters Of War*, and more recently, *Dr Strangelove*? I think these things do have an effect. At least, they're a place to put feelings for many people. And you need a place to hang up your feelings, you know."

During the last two years of the Vietnam war, Lacy played nothing but *The Woe*. By chance, it was finally recorded in Switzerland the night before the armistice was signed. He's never played it since.

CAPERS

These days Steve Lacy is a song and dance man.

Song has formed an increasing proportion of his work since the mid-70s: he's composed around Buddhist chants, Chinese love poems and Braque's notebooks. He met Brion Gysin in Paris in 1974, and their collaboration received its fullest expression so far on the joint *Songs* lp of 1981.

Lacy's most recent album is *Ballets*, which includes a solo set he performed with dancer Pierre Droulers. Was this interest in dance a new direction for him?

"Yes and no. I think jazz was, is, and will be, dance music. That's how it began, that New Orleans music was dance music. And even up through the bebop, people were still dancing to Art Blakey and Horace Silver. To me, it never stopped, it's always been going on.

"Now that's one kind of dancing, and the ballet and modern dance is another. We've been doing a lot of work with dancers in France, and I think there's something a little bit new coming up."

What about if people just got up and danced at your gigs?

"It's a dream, it's a dream of mine." He chuckles. "The first time I played with Cecil Taylor, the first job he called me up for in 1953, that was for a dance. We worked quite a few dances, playing, like, Monk tunes, standards, show tunes; some originals too, but with a beat, with tempos the dancers would like. I got to enjoy it a lot."

Lacy may enjoy dance music, but his dislike of rock is well-known. "It's thin, tame stuff," he groans.

Explain yourself.

"I think jazz is *daring*. Right from the early stuff, like Louis Armstrong, jazz was audacious in form, in everything. It took chances and broke the rules.

"Rock is just a piece of that, a fascination with the beat, it eliminates most of the danger. Look, I grew up with boogie woogie, and if you hear Albert Ammons, Meade Lux Lewis, even Jelly Roll Morton, if you hear the swing and invention and power of that music, how can you take rock seriously? No, I can't go for it, it either sends me to sleep or makes my head hurt."

Lacy adds, though, that this aversion applies mostly to post-60s music. Back in the 60s, before, as he says, the music was "narrowed down" to *rock*, he was a fan of The Beatles, Stevie Wonder, Jimi Hendrix.

"Hendrix was one of my idols. To me, he was one of the gods, and that's the only name that'll go because he played like nobody's business. It was beyond all the categories, and that's the kinda stuff I like, stuff that transcends those earthly categories.

"Hell with the rest of it, the most interesting thing in music is the magic. That's what we're after – pure magic."

TIPS

"Stravinsky said the most important thing for an artist is at what point he can tell all the other artists in the world to go fuck themselves. The sooner he does that, the better."

Lacy laughs. "I read that and I thought, Whew! But it's true. You gotta be tough. I learned that from Cecil, too."

Then, with a handshake and my murmur of thanks, the interview is over. Lacy has an afternoon gig for the ILEA, playing and talking about his music to groups from London schools. Music, he says, should be *clear*: "There's so much murk about, so much pollution in the world."

So how does he see the music going in the 80s?

"Damned if I know. I just hope we make it to the 90s, that's all."

If we do, Steve Lacy will be leading the way. By following it.

November 1982

CECIL TAYLOR
Invisible At All Times

1. "The Invisible Man is coming! The Invisible Man!" (H.G. Wells)

The face is hidden. A dark blue hat, tight over the skull, flares into a floppy brim that shades the cheeks and overhangs the dark glasses, which reach down almost to the Zapata moustache.

The only bits of the face I can see are the tips of the nose and the chin.

Is it really him?

This elfin figure that moves with a feline grace and speaks in a quiet purr, as fastidious with his language as he is with his dapper dress – is this really the great misunderstood genius of modern jazz, the most awesome pianist in the world?

If it is, why is he giving me such a hard time?

"Hmm, this grapefruit is *bitter*," declares Cecil Taylor. "It's like life, *bitter*!" He leans towards me. "Are we not forgetting your interview? Proceed."

My interview is not going well. We're lunching in a hotel restaurant, and the conversation is constantly interrupted by a stream of waiters bringing bits and pieces of food and cutlery. Even more frustrating, Taylor counters every question I ask by asking me to define what I mean.

I decide that a brief, factual inquiry about his own record label, Unit Core, is a pretty harmless way to proceed. How wrong I am.

Have you still got your own—

"I have *nothing*!" Taylor exclaims.

Er— your own record label? You set one up?

"No! No, I don't; yes, I do. Somewhere in between lies the truth in that statement." He grins at me.

Ah— so what happened to it?

"Well, I'm not quite sure. What do you mean?" He affects surprise.

Why did you start it, and, if it no longer exists, why did you stop it?

"Well, you see, I'm saying it's somewhere in the middle of all that. It's an imaginary line that's crossing space, right in this room, right now. You wouldn't believe that, would you? Look!" Taylor points dramatically over my shoulder. "There it goes. You see?"

I smile nervously. Taylor pokes at his grapefruit, then looks up.

"But in any case we must struggle vainly, I mean *gloriously*, to scale the heights that no one ever reached. With shoes on or with shoes off. With fingernails or without. In as many different languages as possible. It seems to me that love is the most important thing."

I stare at him incredulously. Am I lunching with a genius or a fruitcake?

"How would I know about love?" Taylor continues softly. "How would you define love, Isio?"

"Huh?" Isio Saba, the affable, leonine Italian who's managing Taylor's European tour, looks up from the large beef salad he's happily munching.

"Oh, Isio, you're not listening to us," Taylor purrs. "Do *you* believe in love?" he asks me.

Er, yes, I venture apprehensively.

"You do? How extraordinary! Why? How would you *define* this love?"

My heart sinks. Well, I say, I think it's indefinable.

"Why is that? How do you know it exists if you can't define it?"

You can *feel* it.

"What does *that* mean?" Taylor persists. "What is it that you experience when you are *feeling* something? Is that not a fair question?" he adds innocently.

Yes. No. I don't know. I flounder in irritation. Taylor *knows* all about feeling; one of his most famous quotes is that "to feel is the most terrifying thing one can do in this society". Look, I say, it's you the readers want to find out about, not me.

He arches his eyebrows. "Is it not possible for them to find out something about me by the way I answer your questions by asking you other questions?"

Possibly, I say, desperately trying to remember what *my* question was.

"But you still haven't answered my question," he insists. "How do you know that you're alive? How do I know that I'm eating this grape? Hmm, the grapes are good. Want one?"

He offers me a bunch of fat, black grapes and I pick one off with shaking fingers. How can Cecil Taylor *not* know he's being a prize pain in the neck?

"Don't be shy, take several," urges Taylor. "I think I'm a very generous guy, but I might be wrong. Who knows? Isio, what do you think?"

"Huh?" Isio is again disturbed from his beef salad.

Taylor chuckles. "Isio is being very philosophical today. *I'm* the one who has to be philosophical because *I'm* the one that's in jeopardy.

"Did you know that?" he demands. "That artists are always in jeopardy, that we're out there alone, we're beacons of light in the most desolate blankness ever existing in the life of mankind. Ha ha ha. You don't believe that?"

Why do it then, if it's *so* difficult? I make an irked attempt at sarcasm.

"I don't *do* anything at all," Taylor hisses gently. "I simply have found a way of existence that is very satisfactory for me. I live for my self-preservation. That's about all I can really tell you.

"My life is an open book." He smiles and opens his palms towards me. "The reason it's open is because there are no pages in it."

2. *"I am invisible, understand, simply because people refuse to see me."*
(Ralph Ellison)

Of all the musicians living today, few have had to face the hostility, abuse and incomprehension accorded Cecil Taylor.

Back in the 50s, critics denied that his work even counted as *music*; when he joined in jam sessions, other players would pack up and walk out. On one of the rare occasions that he played in a nightclub, bassist Buell Neidlinger recalls: "After about eight bars of Cecil's piano, the owner came running up and told him to get out of the club. He wouldn't even let us finish one song."

Taylor is now acknowledged as one of the architects of modern jazz, on a par with Ornette Coleman and John Coltrane, and his phenomenal piano technique is unequalled in any sphere of music. But the abuse still continues. Just last year a long-established jazz journal claimed that Taylor sounded like a monkey doodling on the keyboard. Thirty years of racist jibes leave their mark: life gets *bitter*.

Cecil Taylor was born in Long Island, New York, in 1933. His was a musical family; his father sang the blues, his mother played piano and violin. Taylor began piano lessons at the age of six; by the time he was nine, he was writing his own music.

He studied at the New York College of Music and the New England Conservatory in Boston, a formal training which some critics have cited in 'identifying' a European avant-garde influence in his music. Taylor, though, has played down this influence, pointing out that he never got to study composition at Boston because a racist teacher wouldn't allow him into the class.

He places himself firmly in the *black* tradition of music, naming Fats Waller, Erroll Garner, Bud Powell, Horace Silver, Thelonious Monk and Duke Ellington as his sources of inspiration.

In fact, Sonny Greer, the great Ellington drummer, was a family friend; and one of Taylor's early jobs was with a combo led by Ellington's alto saxist Johnny Hodges. "It was the greatest thing that ever happened to me," Taylor told critic Nat Hentoff in 1958, "the next best thing to sitting in the Ellington band."

Ironically, Taylor was so nervous he could barely play, and five days after he joined the band he was sacked.

It was at this time – the mid 50s – that Taylor began to work out his own musical ideas; and in the decade which followed the release of his debut lp, *Jazz Advance* for Transition in 1956 (the first example of the 'new jazz' to get onto record), he became the most revolutionary and controversial talent of the era.

He was offered few recording dates, but those lps he did make, like *Looking Ahead!, The World Of Cecil Taylor, Into The Hot, Nefertiti The Beautiful One Has Come, Unit Structures* and *Conquistador*, have become vital markers in the evolution of jazz. Many of his sidemen – Steve Lacy, Sunny Murray, Archie Shepp, Henry Grimes – went on to become leading voices in their own right. (More recent Taylor graduates include Sam Rivers, Andrew Cyrille and Ronald Shannon Jackson.)

Though a technical innovator – he was the first notable figure to introduce atonality into jazz – Taylor's profound impact on musicians touched deeper levels. Eric Dolphy *dreamed* of being ready to play with Taylor, and also dreamed he would die before it could happen.

His friend Jeanne Phillipe told A.B. Spellman: "It was the weirdest thing. Before Eric went to Europe he told me about a dream he had had. He dreamt he was on the bandstand with Cecil— and he was waiting for his turn to play. He said he kept saying to himself, at last I'm going to play with Cecil. And before he could play, he fell down dead on the bandstand. This was the last time I talked to him before he went to Europe, and the next thing I heard, Eric had died— in Berlin."[1]

Albert Ayler, then an obscure saxophonist wandering through Europe, heard Taylor play at Montmartre in 1962 and leapt to his feet, shouting "I finally found somebody I can play with! Please let me play!" Taylor did hire him later and the two played together a few times back in the States. But gigs were hard to come by and, thanks to the racist obduracy of the US music business, no recording was ever made of this unique musical pairing.

Taylor had trouble hustling any kind of gig: a couple of week-long engagements plus the odd festival were his yearly average. So he played dances and took a string of menial jobs to make ends meet – one, particularly galling, was as a dishwasher in a trendy restaurant that regularly played his records over the PA.

Because he was black, articulate and *serious* about his music, nightclub owners shunned him. As Buell Neidlinger told A.B. Spellman, "They want to sell drinks. But when Cecil's playing, people are likely to tell the waiter to shut up and be still."

Pianos were another problem for Taylor. He is a hard, physical player, which means his piano needs to be retuned, and keys perhaps replaced, after every performance. But, to quote Neidlinger again, "You know club owners – they couldn't give a damn about how in tune the piano is. Like, there's a piano there, you play it."

The result was that a man whom many consider the world's greatest pianist had to spend years playing only on beat-up bar-room uprights.

When times were really hard, only Taylor's last-ditch determination pulled him through. According to Nat Hentoff, "I remember him telling me once – after he had been out of work for months – that he had been playing in his room for an imaginary audience. He needed that contact, even if it was just in his head, to re-energise his will to keep on keeping on."

In 1965, by which time he'd been playing music for nearly 15 years, Taylor remarked that he'd yet to earn enough money in a year to have to pay income tax. At one point, he became so enraged at the conditions in which black artists had to work that he called for "a boycott by Negro musicians of all jazz clubs in the United States— let's take the music away from the people who control it".

That call went unheeded; but Taylor was also involved in musicians' organisations such as the Jazz Composers' Guild and the Jazz And People's Movement, both part of the wave of radical politics that swept through jazz in the 60s, and they *did* achieve a limited success in winning due reward for their members' work.

It wasn't until the 1970s, though, that Cecil Taylor at last found a modicum of financial security. He became a Visiting Professor at the University of Madison in Wisconsin and later spent two years with his regular trio – saxist Jimmy Lyons and drummer Andrew Cyrille – as Artists in Residence at Antioch College, Ohio.

But even his academic tenure was turbulent: one year he caused a rumpus by failing nearly all his students for not trying hard enough, and the college authorities, no doubt nervous for their reputation, stepped in to upgrade them all.

Though there are no recordings of Taylor's music for the years 1963-65 and 1970-72, his recent work has been relatively well documented: there are group records from 1976, 1978 and 1980 and a superb series of solo lps from 1973-1981, including *Indent, Silent Tongues, Air Above Mountains, Fly! Fly! Fly! Fly! Fly!* and *Garden*, that confirm Taylor's status as one of the leading composers, improvisers and performers of the current jazz age.

But if Taylor has found life easier in recent years, his native America still accords him less recognition than Europe. Most of his lps in the 70s and 80s have been released on European labels such as Enja, MPS and Hat Hut. The latter in particular, with its top quality recording and pressing standards, has treated Taylor's work with the care it deserves.

The label's reward has been three of his best lps: the fiery ensemble blows of *It Is In The Brewing Luminous* and *One Too Many Salty Swift And Not Goodbye* and –especially – the brilliant solo set *Garden*, perhaps the most scintillating, majestic music Taylor has yet made. Its breathless beauty and daring is a dervish dance along the outer limits of jazz; 100 minutes of rapturous, rampant genius.

3. *"We try to be invisible at all times, even during interviews."* (Cecil Taylor)

Cecil Taylor once said that "anybody's music is made up of a lot of things that are not musical. Music is an attitude, a group of symbols of a way of life."

So I ask him what non-musical things make up his music.

"I don't remember saying that. Jesus, that was pretty good," he muses. "But that was the other me."

The other you?

"Yes. Now I'm an artist with a swollen finger." He holds out his left forefinger. Between the nail and the top knuckle the skin is taut and angry pink over an eruption of pus. "I'm on the verge of a great tragedy," he sighs. "My finger is swollen. Can I go on tonight?"

I try rephrasing my question. Do you ever try to incorporate external events in your music like, say, Steve Lacy's 'The Woe' was a response to the Vietnam war? Is there anything like that you try to *deal with* in the music?

"Just getting up every day," Taylor smiles.

That's it?

"Well, you know, if you are alive and open to situations, you have the whole materialist world to deal with – and that simply means that things of the spirit are not thought to be important, because they can't be *seen*. So we try to be invisible at all times, even during interviews."

He picks at his salad. "I mean, if you make a commitment to beauty, then everything becomes material which can be used— That wasn't said too well." He pauses for thought.

"See, the situation that we continually run into is a misunderstanding of what this music is really about. This piece 'Children In Air', which I'm working on now, is involved with three things which are preoccupations of mine.

"The whole search in life, it seems to me, is to find out who one is: historically, in an investigation of one's religion, and, uh, searching for a kind of language – in writing words, in speaking – a language that could only be defined by its poetic essence.

"'Children In Air' combines poems, ritualised chants, references to American Indians, to voodoo, and it becomes important because American culture, as I perceive it, is *that*."

He breaks off to sip his tea. "Bleah! He's put enough honey in here to drown a whale. Shit, it's terrible!— I'm sorry, you want to ask me another question?"

Presumably, you find it easier to get work now than you did in the 50s and 60s?

Taylor stares at me. "Whoever works, whoever worked, is unlucky, unfortunate, a victim, dispossessed of a privacy related to the time continuum that is, after all, all we have, which is life. So I don't work. Who wants to work? I don't work, I never have. I don't like the idea of lifting anything. Sometimes I lift my feet, but then it's simply that I trip the light fantastic."

Ho hum, here we go. Luckily, I remember that Taylor is not only an expert on ballet and modern dance, but also has a reputation – at the age of 50 – for being a *very* nifty disco dancer.

So what's your favourite dance record? I ask. To my surprise, I get an enthusiastic reply.

"There's a track on Marvin Gaye's new record, I think it's the first track on side two, which is *really* vintage Marvin Gaye. I *love* to dance to that."

4. *"Listening to Cecil is a catharsis – an onrush of emotional hailstorms,*

sunshowers, great winds, cunning breezes, forest fires, avalanches."
(Nat Hentoff)

Cecil Taylor's most famous description of his playing style – "I try to imitate on the piano the leaps in space a dancer makes" – suggests a source for both the *dramatic* quality of his music and its rhythmic core. Other people hear other metaphors: critics Gary Giddins and Val Wilmer have noted the *percussive* elements of Taylor's playing – the latter describing his keyboard as "88 tuned drums" – while Buell Neidlinger has remarked on Taylor "trying to get the vocal sound out of the piano – you can almost hear the piano scream or cry".

Taylor has also spoken of yet another approach: "I try to think of the piano as an orchestra", and voiced a wish "to get colours out of sound the way Ellington did".

The common thread in these analogies – dance, drums, vocal and orchestral textures – is their *physicality*, a quality which Taylor sees as *the* basic component of the black tradition.

He draws a contrast with the lightness of touch admired in both white jazz and European classical music, saying acidly of one well-known pianist "he's so detached he ain't even there", and allying himself, at least implicitly, with that less respectful approach represented by Willie 'The Lion' Smith, who boasted he could "play Chopin faster than any man alive".

"We in Black music think of the piano as a percussive instrument," Taylor told Val Wilmer in her book *As Serious As Your Life*. "We beat the keyboard, we get inside the instrument— the physical force going into the making of Black music – if that is misunderstood, it leads to screaming—"[2]

Just *how* physical Taylor's playing can be was related to Val Wilmer by drummer Rashied Ali, who invited Taylor to break in a secondhand piano he'd just bought: "He sat at the piano and we played from about 12 at night close to about five in the morning. Straight through without let up. Every now and then I would look over at the piano, and Cecil would make like a run down the piano, man, and the keys would be shooting out of the piano like bullets! They were just flying past me— I had to get a whole new set of keys, but he really broke that piano in for me."

Taylor's stamina is as phenomenal as his technique. Five-hour rehearsals are a common, almost a daily, occurrence; and his sets rarely last for less than two hours, yet another bone of contention with club owners.

The day I interview Taylor, he devotes the afternoon to a two-hour, non-stop rehearsal, still playing even while he confers with the rest of the band, his hands scampering up and down the keyboard as if with a life of their own. A little later in the evening comes the two-hour, non-stop performance. After the gig, Taylor is so exhausted he has to be helped to his car.

This ability to give his *all* is part of his genius. As he told A.B. Spellman back in 1966, "When James Brown goes into his thing, he goes— Every fucking thing goes and there ain't no holding back. And it's beautiful."

5. *"'Well! I've often seen a cat without a grin,' thought Alice, 'but a grin without a cat! It's the most curious thing I ever saw in my life!'"* (Lewis Carroll)

"This food is abysmal." Cecil Taylor pushes his salad aside with a quiet groan and looks around for a waiter. "Could you bring the fruit trolley, please?"

The waiter scowls at Taylor's half-eaten salad. "Have you had your main course yet?"

"Oh yes, I've finished."

"You've finished? When you're ready, sir, when *everybody's* ready," he glares meaningfully at Isio Saba, contentedly munching his beef salad, "*then* we'll bring the sweet around."

"OK," Taylor shrugs.

"Unless you're in a hurry." The waiter grudgingly plays out his role.

"As you like." Taylor's voice hardens into a steely sarcasm.

"As *you* wish, sir," the waiter sneers.

"I'm ready now, actually." Taylor's smile is knife-sharp.

"Then I'll fetch the fruit trolley." The waiter flounces off.

Taylor shakes his head. "You see the games we have to go

through. You chuckle? I thought you were a *serious* journalist."

To oblige, I try another serious question. Suppose, I say, an unknown black musician is playing a new kind of jazz in the US now, would it be as hard for him or her as it was for you? Is the establishment still against innovators?

"You've answered your own question. The minute you say 'establishment', that really tells you everything."

So things are as bad as they ever were?

Taylor leans across the table towards me and speaks with a quiet insistence. "The music is simply *not* encouraged. Its growth is not encouraged, its place in the American culture is ignored, there is no *real* information made available as to the aesthetic principle within the structure of sound.

"One could say that, given the world recognition of the kind of constructions that black Americans have given the world, for it *not* to be enshrined in America is the indication that the establishment has problems dealing with the rituals involved.

"It is, if anything, *more* difficult today to find one's centre, because of all the defections within the music, the perpetual mountain of false idols, the propagating of values attendant on the most *shallow*: and because of the menial attitudes of most executives in the music, the refusal of these men to recognise anything beyond their economic reasoning – which at the same time allows them to assault the integrity of some of the most creative people in the world – indeed, in this area, this music, *the* most creative.

"It is always an *embarrassment* to realise that one has to live in spite of perpetual harassment, and it's at a point where their insensitivity is simply *there* – they don't even recognise their inability to think, feel—

"It is an *embarrassment* too, because there's nothing you can do about it. We do it in spite of— for our resistance, and we get better, too. Because, as Abbey Lincoln said, the music is like the earth: the more you shit upon it, the more fertile the earth becomes. And, like, the more they try to defecate upon us, the richer we become."

Taylor leans back in his chair, and suddenly grins. "Well, did you like that? The last part was pretty good, huh?"

This is the image I retain of Cecil Taylor: mocking, elusive; the mind-dance behind the mask of shades and inscrutable smile.

Taylor playing in full flow is the most spectacular sound in music, a crashing torrent of passion and power, the fastest, hardest, most relentless playing imaginable. Yet he is also capable of great delicacy, a richness of melody, the emotional resonance of the blues. A complete piano genius. To quote Buell Neidlinger, "That man is capable of playing ten different notes with ten different fingers, ten different dynamics, ten different attacks, and at least ten different tempi."

"Oh God, how can I play with *this*?" He stares at his swollen finger in dismay. "Can I go on tonight? Isio, can I go on?"

Isio looks up from his salad with a serene smile. "Of course-a you can. Is there anything better for the artist than-a dying over the piano?"

"But so soon!" Cecil Taylor exclaims softly. "I've just begun to live."

March 1983

1. This and later quotes are from A.B. Spellman's *Four Lives In The Bebop Business* (New York: Limelight, 1985).
2. Val Wilmer, *As Serious As Your Life* (London: Pluto Press, 1987).
The various Nat Hentoff quotes, incidentally, are mostly from his numerous, and invaluable, lp sleeve-notes.

MAL WALDRON
Waltzing With Fire

Mal Waldron looks up from his cup of coffee and suddenly announces, "Did you know Ella Fitzgerald has just married Darth Vader?"

Huh? What's that?

"Yeah, now she's called Ella Vader!"

He chuckles quietly, while photographer Val Wilmer and I exchange bemused glances. I come to hear about jazz in the melting pot from one of the hottest talents of the era, and I get – *Ella Vader*.

One hour later, I realise I'm lucky to get that. As the interview peters to an end in Waldron's tiny hotel room, I make a last attempt to draw him out.

Look, I say, the late 50s/early 60s were a special time for jazz.

"Definitely," he assents. "Very special."

And you were *there*. You played with the greatest musicians of the time – Billie Holiday, John Coltrane, Charles Mingus, Eric Dolphy – and you became a major figure yourself. So what particular memories do you have of those days? What stands out?

"Ah, let me see. It's a little hazy."

Waldron frowns with concentration and lights up another of the dark, elegant cigarettes that he chain smokes. Long pause.

"I can't really think of anything particular, it was just a very productive time for me. I worked hard and earned a lot." He laughs apologetically. "I'm not really into anecdotes."

Oh, well. Thanks anyway, Mal.

"Thank *you*, Brian."

He's right, of course. You'd have to be crazy to blurt out your fondest memories to a nosy stranger with a tape recorder, who'll likely as not twist and trivialise them all over the pages of some trashy newspaper. Still, it's a shame Mal Waldron is *so* reticent – as he says himself, "I'm not a verbal person" – because he's a man with a headful of history.

He was *there*: with Billie Holiday the night she sang her last song; with John Coltrane as he began his revolutionary reshaping of jazz; with the doomed duo of Eric Dolphy and Booker Little for their legendary two-week stay at New York's Five Spot; with Max Roach and Abbey Lincoln as they gave first voicings to the black pride and black anger that swept a jazz generation – in each case that shy guy in the shadows on piano was Mal Waldron.

There's more, too. A filmscore for Marcel Carne, music for the plays of LeRoi Jones; and Mal Waldron lps launched the ECM, Enja *and* Futura record labels. (He was also the man who, via his album *The Quest*, with Eric Dolphy, turned this particular fan onto jazz.)

But Mal Waldron is not just a history man. He has steadily grown into one of the most distinctive and subtle of modern pianists, as well as a leading composer and improviser. If he remains somewhat underrated by the critics, it's partly because he's been living in 'exile' in Europe since 1965 – and it's still the American media that tend to make jazz reputations – and partly due to the self-effacing personality which spills over into his piano style.

His music may, as he claims, speak for him; but it does so with the same economy of means, the same disavowal of rhetoric, that marks his conversation. It's a musical approach he once attributed to growing up in hard times: "We were never rich people and never threw anything away. So when I have a note I make full use of it, milk it in every possible way."

The result is a music that slowly draws you in, eschewing extrovert pyrotechnics for a kind of musing aloud, a rigorous 'wringing dry' of simple motifs which he takes through many moods – sombre rumblings to crisp exuberance to rhapsodic waltzes – before discarding them as spent.

Malcolm Earl Waldron was born on 16 August 1925 in New York City. His parents were West Indian immigrants, and though they encouraged his music – he began playing piano at the age of eight – it was strictly classical; jazz, they said, was "the devil's music". But that didn't stop the young Mal tuning the radio to a jazz station and exulting, when his parents were out, to the sounds of swing: Symphony Sid, The Savoy Sultans, Ben Webster, Lester Young. When he heard Coleman Hawkins play 'Body And Soul', he heard his destiny call.

He bought an alto sax ("I couldn't afford a tenor") and began to blow with a neighbourhood swing band. Later, he reverted to piano because the band needed a stronger pianist, and finally abandoned his sax ambitions when he heard Charlie Parker play.

"I first heard him in, I think, 1945, playing 'Hot House'. When the Dial records came out I took my sax to the nearest hock shop. I knew it was a lost cause."

Waldron persisted as a jazz pianist, absorbed bebop, and worked his way up through the jungle of local and semi-name bands. His first gig with a big name came in 1950 with tenorist Ike Quebec, and he made his recording debut then too, on a 78 called 'Kiss Of Fire'. In 1954 he met Charles Mingus, and what Waldron calls "the snowball effect" really began to roll.

Through working in Mingus' experimental Jazz Workshop – notably on the *Pithecanthropus Erectus* lp – he met saxist Jackie McLean and through him he got a gig with Prestige Records, one of the major jazz labels of the 50s. Prestige liked him, and he became a member of the house rhythm section, which meant not only recording with some of the best horns around – John Coltrane, Charlie Rouse, Pepper Adams, Gene Ammons, Art Farmer – but also writing and arranging the music for many of the sessions.

Then, in April 1957, came an offer he couldn't refuse. Billie Holiday had a gig in Philadelphia, but no pianist: the news went down the grapevine and Waldron jumped at the chance.

"The buck stopped with me," he laughs. "I said, Yeah I'll do it, and the next day I left for Philadelphia."

Waldron stayed with Billie Holiday for nearly two and a half years, until her death in June 1959. As well as being her accompanist, he became a close friend and she was godmother to his first daughter. I ask the inevitable question: what was she like?

"Fantastic, fantastic." Waldron nods his head appreciatively. "She was like a big sister to me. She was very helpful, very kind, very warm, very loving. I just grew with her. It was a beautiful experience, very educational."

How 'educational'?

"I learned about the importance of words, to think of melodies in terms of words, which gives you an added basis on which to build your solos. It's like a whole new emotion to explore while you're soloing."

She was ill a lot at that time, wasn't she?

"Yeah, but that didn't really affect her performance." Waldron pauses to light a cigarette. "Up on stage she wasn't sick, she'd sing and do her thing, and when she was finished she might come off stage and feel a little sick."

(There are records which argue otherwise, but let's not go into that.)

I read a quote of yours where you said that had Billie Holiday settled in Europe, she'd be living today.

"Definitely she'd be alive, because the attitude towards drugs in Europe then was that it was not a crime, it was a sickness, and they would try to help you get better. But in America it was considered a crime, so you were treated like a criminal, and this attitude towards drugs is what killed Billie Holiday.

"She died from an overdose of police, so to speak, not an overdose of drugs. There was just too much police pressure on her, and that made her give up the ghost."

Do you think there was an element of racism in that police pressure?

"Definitely. If they caught two junkies together, one white and one black, like the white one might get a slap across the wrist, but the black one would get a truncheon across the head."

So Billie Holiday died her infamous death. Busted in a hospital room, she was forcibly fingerprinted and photographed as she lay helpless by detectives who, in an act of gratuitous malice, also removed from her room her flowers, books, record-player and radio. She died within a few weeks, a police guard still sitting outside her door.

She was 44 years old.

Mal Waldron later released two lps in tribute to Billie Holiday: *Blues For Lady Day* and *Left Alone*, the latter named after the poignant ballad which she co-wrote with him, and which, she told him, was "the story of my life".

Perhaps the best recorded version of 'Left Alone' is on Abbey Lincoln's *Straight Ahead* lp from 1961, which features Waldron with drummer Max Roach, reedsman Eric Dolphy and trumpeter Booker Little, the three musicians with whom he was to enjoy fruitful, if brief, associations in the early 60s.

After Billie Holiday's death, he worked a while with Lincoln, then with her husband, the great bebop drummer and political radical Max Roach, playing on lps such as *Speak, Brother, Speak* and the controversial *Percussion Bitter Sweet* (also with Dolphy and Little), which honoured Marcus Garvey, Civil Rights, Women's Liberation and South African freedom fighters at a time when such honour could get you banned from American recording studios – and, sure enough, Max Roach was not able to record again for five years.

Waldron also played in Roach's and Lincoln's spectacular staging of their 'We Insist! Freedom Now Suite', one of *the* live events in early 60s New York; and with Eric Dolphy and Booker Little at their now-famous two-week season at the Five Spot in July 1961, one night of which was released as a Prestige three-lp set, *The Great Concert Of Eric Dolphy*.

The record became a memorial for both Little, who died later that year, aged 23, and also for Dolphy, who died in 1964 at the age of 36.

"That was a very intense fortnight," Waldron recalls quietly, lighting up another cigarette. "You had two very strong forces there, Booker Little and Eric Dolphy. They were both driven by the unconscious knowledge that they wouldn't be here long."

You really felt that?

"Yeah. I think it happens, on an unconscious level, that you know you're not going to be here long, so you rush to get everything done. They were both very intense people, they worked and practised all the time, didn't take any breaks, as if they knew they didn't have long to get it done. Same thing with Coltrane, he just didn't take the horn out of his mouth."

Waldron was still recording for Prestige, and a few days before the Five Spot gig he took Dolphy into the studio to help out on his sixth lp, *The Quest*. History may remember the record chiefly for Dolphy's rare Bb clarinet solo on 'Warm Canto', but it will always retain a special place in my affections as the lp which first opened my ears to jazz; and 'Warm Canto' and the ravishing 'Fire Waltz' still come high on my list of favourite jazz tracks.

Waldron smiles when I tell him this.

"Well, you know, I wrote all the songs the night before the session. I stayed up all night to write the tunes and arrange them, so when I got to the gig I was very tired, but the spirit of the musicians was so strong, it carried me along."

Why this last-minute rush?

"I was so busy. I wrote the music to pretty much all of the Prestige record dates we were on, so my date was not, like, anything special, just another date I had to write music for. We would do dates every day, maybe two dates, six hours playing, then I'd come home and write the music for the next day. It was a very productive time for me."

I mention that *The Quest* has subsequently been retitled *Fire Waltz* and reissued under Eric Dolphy's name. Waldron laughs.

"That's because he died before me. When I die, I'll get that album back again. In fact, I'll get quite a few albums back." He chuckles, "I won't be able to *use* them then, but that's the way it is in this world – you die, you get the credit."

"Anyway," he adds with a smile, "I still get the royalties."

Some of the people you were working with in the 50s and early 60s, especially Charles Mingus and Max Roach, were very outspoken politically. Were you involved in those radical politics, too?

Waldron nods. "Oh yeah, I was involved. But not in such an outspoken way as they were, because I was not very verbal. But I used my music. Like 'The Call For Arms' is a tune I wrote when the African nations started to emerge, and 'If You Think I'm Licked' was a tune I wrote to encourage the attitude that was coming up.

"But I was not a spokesman like Max Roach. I've always been the shy, retiring type."

Why did you leave America in 1965?

"Because the attitude in America at that time was that the musician, and particularly the black musician, was like the lowest man on the totem pole. The highest man was the white man with lots of money in the bank. And that was their scale of achievement.

"So with an attitude like that, I thought, well, I'm black, I'm a musician, I don't have any money, why should I live in a society that thinks I'm the *worst*, let's get OUT of that society. I came to Europe, and I found the attitude was quite the opposite. They thought the black man was a beautiful person, and that he could play music better than the white man, and they'd give you lots of money, too."

He laughs. "So I stayed in Europe."

He lived in Paris and Bologna before settling in Munich in 1967.

"The German mark was stronger than the franc or the lira, which were up and down like making winky winky," Waldron explains with a grin.

In Europe, he found political freedom, relative financial security and the chance to devote himself entirely to his music. He is now, he says, a happy man.

No feeling of isolation? Eighteen years away from home is a long time.

"No, I don't feel isolated because I carry my culture with me." Waldron taps his chest. "I think every person has their home within them, and wherever you go it goes with you, and that's who you are."

He tours the continent regularly, and also plays a lot in Japan, where he's *the* best-selling jazz recording artist. Munich is also the home of two of Europe's best-known jazz labels, ECM and Enja, both of which Waldron, in his role as local 'big name' artist, helped to launch. He still releases most of his records on Enja, and through the 70s and 80s has built up an impressive catalogue – lps such as *Black Glory, Free At Last, A Touch Of The Blues, Hard Talk, Moods, Mingus Lives, What It Is, One Entrance, Many Exits, Snake Out* – which shows him developing, in solo, trio and group contexts, an increasingly freer approach to his music.

It's a musical journey which, he says, he began with Coltrane and Dolphy, who taught him "the possibilities of playing *outside* of the structure", and has continued in Europe, notably with soprano saxist Steve Lacy, with whom he made what he considers to be his first totally free lp in 1971, *Mal Waldron With The Steve Lacy Quintet*.

It's to play a concert with Lacy, another mid-60s American exile, that Mal Waldron is now in London, renewing a partnership that goes back more than 20 years, to an lp of Monk tunes called *Reflections* that, by chance, has just been reissued by Fantasy records.

But although it was a love of Monk that brought the pair together, the man whom Waldron credits with most influencing his piano style is bassist Charles Mingus.

"From Mingus I learned the way to play the piano. Because he was a pianist too, and he would demonstrate tunes to us on piano. He didn't want us to learn his music from written notes, he wanted us to learn it by rote, because that way he felt we'd never forget it.

"And I watched him play the piano, and his voicings were fantastic and beautiful, and he played the full scope of the piano, with elbows and all!"

So, I ask, what's your aim in music now? You've been through swing, bebop and free – what's left?

"Well, uh, I'm just trying to get freer and freer, really." Waldron exhales a stream of cigarette smoke. "Trying to throw away all the things that restrict me. Like, harmony and rhythm, they're about the only things that restrict me now. Form doesn't and melody doesn't, but, like, I'm so aware of harmonic structure that whenever I play free I still go through the harmonic changes that are based on older music. But I just want to play emotionally."

Emotionally?

"For example, I should be able to describe what's happening today, to react on an emotional level, without it having a form, or being rhythmically recurrent, or having a harmonic base. You should just use *sound*, like – WAAAAAAAAAUUUUUUUUGGGGHHHHHHH!"

Waldron lets loose a bellow like an elephant in extreme distress. Good God, I think, if that's how he's feeling I better get out of here and leave him in peace.

One last question then, Mal. Are you getting there? Free at last?

"I think it's coming, but it doesn't happen to me very suddenly. I'm a slow developer." He chuckles. "That's why I feel I'm gonna have a long life, 'cause they gotta give me time to get it all worked out. The people who work it out fast, like Eric Dolphy or John Coltrane or Clifford Brown, they *go* fast. They gotta die young, 'cause there's nothing left for them to do.

"I'm gonna be around a long time 'cause I haven't worked it out yet. They'll have to leave me down here until I do."

Mal Waldron is one of the quiet men of jazz, but his reticence shouldn't mislead us into undervaluing his achievements.

In the early days of modern jazz, he was in the crucial places at the crucial times, and his subsequent body of work gloriously confirms his stature as a major jazz talent. He may not produce fireworks but look under that bushel and you'll find a slowburner with a steady flame.

A little later, we end the interview and Waldron returns with a sigh of relief to the computer chess game, which is his constant travelling companion. My efforts to delve into his past must have been something of an ordeal for such a shy man, but he remains politely amenable to the end.

And then, at his ICA gig that night, he gives me a kind of present. Or, at least, I think he does. His set ends, but after a quick consultation with the MC he comes back and, to my surprise and utter delight, plays a brief, bewitching version of 'Fire Waltz'.

After that, I no longer care that he called me Brian. I may even forgive *Ella Vader*.

August 1983

ABDULLAH IBRAHIM

In Struggle, In Grace

1. THE CULTURAL FREEDOM FIGHTER

"Hit and run, hit and run, freedom comes through the barrel of a gun."

July 1983. Abdullah Ibrahim stands at his hotel room window and looks down at the green turf of the nearby Lords cricket ground.

"Did you see that Australian team?" he asks. "Ray Lindwall, Keith Miller: oooeee, they were *great!*"

You saw them here? I ask, puzzled.

"No, no. In Capetown, in the 50s. I used to watch the cricket there. I saw Stanley Matthews, too." He smiles at the memory of a pleasure long since sacrificed in the fight for that single, elemental right of equality.

It's a minor irony of fate that Abdullah Ibrahim, one of music's most eloquent opponents of apartheid, is here in a hotel overlooking Lords in the very week that the MCC are to vote on whether to send a cricket team to South Africa.

The notion that it's now OK to do so, that the Pretoria regime is taking a more 'liberal' stand on apartheid, is dismissed by Ibrahim with a contemptuous snort.

"It's a joke, man, a smokescreen. What do they actually *mean* by liberal changes? They say, OK, they're going to give limited civil rights to the so-called Coloured people and the so-called Indian people. *Blacks* are completely excluded! That's 75, 80 per cent of the population excluded!

"And Black people didn't vote for this situation," he chuckles incredulously. "So it's illegal – the South African government is *illegal*. I never voted for apartheid. I've never voted in my life."

He lowers his tall, wiry frame into an armchair and pours out two cups of his favourite mu tea. My impression is of a man of great dignity, authority and charm. On the drive back from the soundcheck he was affable, full of humorous anecdotes; now, talking about the politics of his native land, his speech is quiet and urgent.

I ask him how he sees the current situation in South Africa.

"The Nationalist Party are split. Some think they should give these rights, others say that it's opening up the floodgates. And, really, they've created a situation – apartheid – that's impossible for them to dismantle, so they are politically bankrupt. There's nothing that the regime can offer the people, except oppression. It's an instrument of destruction, so it has to be destroyed!"

But how long will that take?

"Time is not the question," Ibrahim says firmly. "Revolution is not, like, OK, let's get it together tonight and tomorrow everything is cool. Revolution is a 24-hour-a-day, 25-hour-a-day job. You have to be watchful. We're not fighting the regime because we want to have a good time; it's for our children and their children. Because my great grandfather fought them, my grandmother, my mother – the people of South Africa have been fighting the fascists for centuries, and we will continue to fight them until they are destroyed. The will of the people *will* prevail, because that is the law.

"Allah says in the Koran, the truth has come and falsehood has vanished. The nature of truth is that it stays, the nature of falsehood is that it leaves."

He smiles grimly. "And the system that regime has created in South Africa must be the most horrendous falsehood ever perpetrated on the human race."

The jazz in this story begins with Louis Jordan and The Tympany Five, whose jump-band music crossed the Atlantic in the 40s and found its way to Capetown, where hits like 'Choo Choo Ch'Boogie', 'Caldonia', and 'Is You Or Is You Ain't My Baby' were blasted out by the township ice-cream vans.

These vans, with their boisterous selections of Jordan, Tiny

Bradshaw, Erskine Hawkins, were a vital source of jazz for the young Abdullah Ibrahim, then Dollar Brand – or, more precisely, Adolph Johannes Brand, born October 1934, son of a Bushman tribeswoman and a Basuto tribesman. The other sources he remembers were the one weekly jazz show on the radio and the musical studies he began at the age of seven, encouraged by a grandmother who played piano at the local AME church.

He began his musical career, though, in a vocal group, The Streamline Brothers (four men, one woman!), whose repertoire spanned South African traditional songs and American doowop.

"Our traditional music," explains Ibrahim, "has the same source as Black American music. The urban music was very close to swing, so it was not like we were playing American music, it was all the same to us. We sang traditional songs, American popular songs, doowop, spirituals— you remember The Deep River Boys?" He breaks off to sing an impromptu version of 'It's Just The Gypsy In My Soul'. "Those Streamline Brothers! Oooeee, they could sing!"

Ibrahim moved to piano for his next band, The Tuxedo Slickers; then came a stint with the Willie Max dance band before, at the beginning of the 60s, he formed his own group, The Jazz Epistles, which included trumpeter Hugh Masekela and altoist Kippie Moeketsi. They were the first Black group in South Africa to record an lp.

What was the government line on jazz then? I ask.

"The government line is that you must stand in line, whatever it is," Ibrahim grunts sarcastically. "At that time the Nationalists had just introduced the Group Areas Act. Before, there were still places where people lived and played together and there were mixed audiences. Then the Nationalists separated everybody into what they thought were their rightful social places, so communication broke down. The whole culture broke down."

Presumably that was one of the reasons you left South Africa in 1962?

"We don't really leave, you know," he says softly. "It's a tactical retreat. We regard ourselves as cultural freedom fighters. And when our cadres, our young people, go outside the country for training, we don't say that they left – it's a tactical retreat."

Abdullah Ibrahim's tactical retreat took him to Switzerland and then around the European club circuit. But it was back in Zurich, in February 1963, that his fiancée Bea Benjamin (now his wife) persuaded an itinerant Duke Ellington to hear him play. Ellington, then a director of Reprise Records, was so impressed that he fixed up some recording dates for the young pianist and supervised them himself.

For Ibrahim, this was a marvellous fillip. Invitations came for him to play at the Antibes Jazz Festival and, in 1965, at the prestigious Newport Jazz Festival. This took him to the US after an unhappy stay in London, which he now remembers as a time of too little work ("I think we got three gigs in six months, two pounds ten shillings a time!") and too much drink ("Oh, man, that was a *foggy* time. The fog was *inside* my head, right? I had a problem then, too much liquid!").

Ibrahim stayed in the US for three years. He played with the Ellington band for a time; he also became very involved in New York's radical music scene, playing with pioneers like John Coltrane, Don Cherry, Ornette Coleman and Sunny Murray.

Was it not a big jump, I ask, from playing with Ellington to playing with, say, Coltrane or Coleman?

"Oh no, man. You've never heard Ellington play 'out'? Wow! Listen to that lp *Piano In The Foreground*. There's a track 'Summertime', listen to Duke's piano there – it's Cecil Taylor!" He grins at my naivety. "They played that stuff *long* ago, it was just never recorded, except here and there, 'cause the record companies freaked out when they heard it.

"It's like the French and Charlie Parker. You know that story? When the critics in America were first writing about Charlie Parker, they sent an lp over to the French critics and the French critics sent it back with a message, whoa, this lp's recorded at the wrong speed. The Americans had to send it back again with a note – no, man, the guy plays at this speed!"

Free music, he adds, was "euphoric to play, but nobody wanted to listen – those were the *lean* years". One consequence of this is that his music in the 70s and 80s has taken several steps back from the farther edges of free-form. Ibrahim still makes room for improvising, but now it's within a song-structure and nearly always balanced by his gift for spare, graceful melodies. If the more avant-garde fans were disappointed, at least a *lot* of people are listening now. Another pertinent factor is that Ibrahim's musical roots predate free-form: John Coltrane was an inspiration, yes, but outside of his African heritage the most evident influences on his music have always been Duke Ellington and Thelonious Monk, whose songs he has frequently recorded.

Why those two in particular? I ask.

He shrugs philosophically. "If you are a so-called European classical player, you have to go through Bach. There's no way you can handle that music without going through Bach. And if you're a pianist you have to dig Chopin. That's Duke and Monk. Monk is an extension of Duke. Duke is the founder and there's no way to get around it. The music of Ellington, the *sound* of Ellington, is an institution. Ellington is the sound scientist, and Monk is – purity and clarity.

"You can play Monk's music to children and they turn on to it immediately. The grown-ups say, whoa, Monk is difficult, he's *weird*, but the reason is *they* are too strung up. Kids listen to him 'cause of that purity and clarity, that angelic quality he kept. And because he's *mischievous*.

"Max Roach told me this story, right. He was recording with Abbey Lincoln, back in the 60s, when Abbey was a very young singer, and this was one of her first lps. She was having trouble with a song, trying and trying to get it right, and Monk was in the studio, just listening. After the fifth or sixth take, he walks over to Abbey and whispers in her ear. And after the session, she says to Max, 'Man, you've got some weird friends. That Monk!' So Max says, 'Why, what did he say?' And she says, 'He came up and he told me, sing it *wrong*!'" Ibrahim bursts into delighted laughter.

"Monk's music is beautiful. You can't get into it or play it without clearing your head. Time! He was into *time*." (He taps out a bop rhythm, then hums a ballad.) "See, Monk played other rhythms too, he played tempos *in between*. That's why drummers had problems with him. Like, you come in there and you're a bebop drummer – pichaw, pichaw, pichaw – but Monk's got one beat that's as big as a house – paaaaaaaaaah – and then it takes a hundred years before the next beat arrives – paaaaaaaaaah! So you've got all this space in between and drummers didn't know what the hell to do, they'd get lost in all that space."

He laughs again. "Like, Monk told Ben Riley once, 'Just because you're the drummer doesn't mean you've got the best beat in the band.' Monk was something else, man!"

In 1968 Abdullah Ibrahim returned to South Africa, and divided the next few years between Africa, Europe and the US. While few of his 60s recordings remain in catalogue, his music through the 70s and 80s has been well documented and lps on numerous labels are currently available in the UK.

Despite the maelstrom of New York free-form from which he'd just emerged, the prime influence on Ibrahim's 70s music was his return to African roots. Nearly every lp title refers to Africa and many individual tracks are either drawn from traditional sources or deal with specific aspects of South African life, often from an upfront political perspective: 'Soweto' and 'Mannenberg' honour the townships, 'Tula Dubula' anticipates the racists' downfall, while 'Hit And Run' baldly asserts *"Freedom comes through the barrel of a gun"*.

These South African songs are the most dramatic element in Ibrahim's music. Whether it's the sombre, left-hand rumbles with which he mourns the latest racist outrage or the exuberant, lyrical swing of his township salutes, there's a direct and deeply emotional quality to his music which can pierce to the heart.

A second vital influence on Ibrahim's work stems from his conversion to Islam in 1968. On lps such as *Good News From Africa* and *Children Of Africa*, the calming presence of Muslim devotional music and chant is to the forefront, and his music's most readily spiritual facet – its sense of serenity – is very apparent.

Though these Afro-Islamic aspects predominate, Ibrahim maintained his interest in the US avant-garde. He spent much of 1972 in Copenhagen, playing with Don Cherry and Carlos Ward (with whom he still works regularly), the fruit of this collaboration being the *Third World-Underground* lp on Trio. He also recorded a couple of breezy big-band lps – *African Space Programme*, *The Journey* – on which New Music luminaries Hamiet Bluiett, Enrico Rava and Sonny Fortune shake the house with their blowing.

Ibrahim, too, was extending his resources, adding soprano sax and flute to his distinctive piano. In recent years he seems to have drawn all these musical strands together, transmuting the separate elements into a new, darting lyricism that's all-pervasive on records like *Zimbabwe* and *Ekaya*. Perhaps because he's now based in New York again, 80s lps such as *Duke's Memories, Zimbabwe* and the solo *African Dawn* show the re-emergence of Ellington and Monk as primary influences, both in the use of their tunes and in what sounds to me like Ibrahim's growing complexity as pianist and composer. His playing is spikier now, the melodies strung with acidic frills: and the swaying grace of 'Sotho Blue' or the sheer, beautiful *rush* of 'For Coltrane No II' reveal a music that's deft, airy, yet richly individual.

His most *sought-after* music, though, dates from the mid-70s: the South African recordings *Soweto* and the legendary *Mannenberg* are still phenomenally popular. It's a bitter irony that, at first, no record company would touch *Mannenburg*.

"What happened with *Mannenberg*," says Ibrahim, his face tensing with anger, "is— like, over the years we've been wanting to record our own music and the record companies have always told us, no, you can't. The record companies are white-controlled, right, so they tell us, the people won't buy this, it's too *primitive*."

Mannenberg was actually recorded during a break in a studio session when Ibrahim began playing around on an old upright piano whose honky tonk sound he liked. When no record company wanted to release that particular tape, Ibrahim made some acetates himself and played the disc in a little record shop near the Johannesburg bus terminal. Within a week, he'd sold 5000 copies over the counter, and the lp, whose appearance had coincided with the 1976 uprisings, became synonymous with the freedom struggle.

In 1976, Ibrahim organised a South African jazz festival that totally contravened government apartheid regulations. A few days later, he slipped out of the country and has never been back. He was, he adds, already in trouble with the authorities for refusing to appear on the country's apartheid tv network – one station for whites, one for Blacks.

"I'm not interested in those divisions," he sighs, "but there's nothing you can do. If you become a commercial success in South Africa, they're going to try to use you, make you pay homage to the system. The moment you become visible, you have no choice. The system drives you into the arms of the revolution: either that or you stop playing. You leave the country or you stop playing. There's no other way to deal with it."

The year 1976, he explains, was a turning point in South African politics.

"The '76 uprising was so widespread, it swept the whole country. It was then that people began to understand that the end of dialogue had come: over 600 people shot dead, unarmed children— so when we left in '76, the ANC asked us to play a more vocal role and we accepted. Dialogue was finished and it seemed to me that the only solution was that we have to free ourselves through armed struggle."

You said earlier that you were a cultural freedom fighter. Can you explain that? What do you see as the *function* of your music in the struggle?

Ibrahim sips his tea thoughtfully, then speaks with a quiet vigour. "You see, the regime calls us terrorists. I look at my mother, she doesn't look like a terrorist to me, a very gentle, very beautiful woman. I look at her, I look at my grandmother, my great grandmother, my great grandfather, I look around and I see my family— you know, Duke Ellington said, 'I was raised in the palm of the hand of the very best people in the land – my mother, my father, and love'. This is where I come from.

"They call *us* terrorists. *We* are being terrorised! Our doors are kicked open at four in the morning and our families dragged off to prison, never to be seen again. We are the ones who are stopped on the streets and asked for pass cards. We are the ones who are not allowed to go to their schools. We are the ones who suffer all these horrors. *They* are the terrorists.

"Now the time has come— our president Oliver Tambo said this year that we have run out of cheeks to turn. That the time has come to say that Black people won't be the only ones to bleed. They call us terrorists, savages, that stereotype. So through the music we can show the *gentleness* of our people – and not just of our people, but of humanity. And the reality, the beauty, of Allah's creation.

"See, you don't have to read about a people or anything," he laughs, "just listen to their music and eat their food. Let the racists play their music and we'll play ours, and you can be the judge."

The day Abdullah Ibrahim flies out of Britain, the MCC vote against sending a cricket team to South Africa. That night on television, I watch a purple-faced Denis Compton, pro-tour spokesman, splutter that a battle has been lost but the war is just beginning. I remember Abdullah's words – "Our people have been fighting the fascists for centuries" – and I know Compton is wrong. This war is an ancient war and, despite Compton or Thatcher or Botha or anyone, the war will be won because it must be won if there is to be any hope or dignity or value in living on this planet.

And I remember the first time I heard Abdullah Ibrahim play live, at Bracknell in 1982. On a late summer afternoon, with the festival marquee packed and keen with expectation, Ibrahim and Carlos Ward played some of the most beautiful and moving music I'll ever hear. By turns delicate, poignant, austere, the duo slipped from Monk to Ellington to traditional African songs, conjuring a resonance from the simplest tune.

As the set reached its climax, the atmosphere grew electric. People wept or punched the air, heads bowed, and yelled ANC slogans. Ward blew a lovely, wailing blues, then Ibrahim sang 'Tula Dubula', a freedom song which moves with gentle inexorability from the grief already paid to the promise of *"a new world a-coming"*. Listening, dazed, to this piercing beauty, I felt my insides lurch and the next moment tears were streaming down my face, all control gone.

The set closed, a flute motif dancing lightly over the piano's grave rumbles, and the whole audience leapt to its feet, drained but ecstatic. The applause came like a cloudburst.

"There's a new world a-coming/Falsehood will all be gone/ They'll come a-marching into town at dawn/Singing songs of freedom and laughing in the rain/Gone will be this old world, things won't be the same."

PART 2: THE MUSIC OF NO MIND

"The eternal spirit is the only reality."

March 1984. At 3pm precisely I knock on the hotel-room door. To my surprise, someone on the inside knocks back. Bemused, I knock again and the door swings open. I step inside to find Abdullah Ibrahim, grinning from ear to ear, hiding behind the door.

"Har!" he exclaims in his guttural, R-rolling accent.

For this meeting I've brought along two friends, musician Katy Zeserson and photographer Nick White, both keen Ibrahim fans. Abdullah, too, has a few mates with him and others drop in during the afternoon, plus more journalists and a constant stream of room-service people bringing teas and fruit juices for the visitors.

The resulting interview is very different from our earlier one. Rather than a sombre analysis of South African politics, the talk today is relaxed and expansive, and revolves mostly around Islam, to which Ibrahim became a convert in 1968 (changing his name from Dollar Brand) and which he discusses in an engaging manner – like the Muslim equivalent of a Zen-master – mixing humour and off-beat anecdotes with the more serious stuff.

We begin talking about his Camden Jazz Week concert of the previous evening. A planned duo with Max Roach had been cancelled the day before the gig when Roach was taken ill, and reedsman Sam Rivers flew in as a last-minute replacement.

Ibrahim and Rivers had not played together before and had little time to rehearse. Was this not a problem? I ask.

Ibrahim frowns for a moment, then smiles. "What did Ben Riley ask Monk? 'Hey, Monk, when are we going to rehearse?' Monk said, 'Why? You wanna learn how to *cheat*?'" He breaks into delighted guffaws, as he will do throughout the afternoon.

You don't rehearse much? asks Katy, when order is restored.

"I don't know where this thing about rehearsal comes from," Ibrahim muses. "I think it comes from the assumption that the things we do are not really in the service of the Almighty. I mean, how are you going to rehearse a prayer? Either you pray or you don't; you don't say 'Hang on, God, I'm gonna have a rehearsal here.' Like, even with a swordsman, every cut he makes is a prayer."

Hmm. I ask how his conversion to Islam had originally come about.

He smiles. "Well, we are all convertible."

But why you? Why then?

"I think we cannot really question the when. That is up to the Creator. All things come through grace, there's nothing you can do about it. We don't make Muslims, you know, Allah makes Muslims. And when you realise that whatever comes to you comes through grace, then you become tolerant. When we do not understand grace, that is the reason we become intolerant."

Katy is still musing on the analogy between rehearsal and prayer. I think a lot of young musicians have the notion that jazz is hard, she says, that you have to practise a lot. Yet your music sounds so simple.

Ibrahim shrugs. "It's like everything, even your religion – if it becomes a burden to you, then you must leave it alone. When you say young musicians think jazz is difficult to play, maybe it's got to do with the interpretation of what technique is.

"For example, we study martial arts and you have to go through the process of practising the basics. But the basic training has nothing to do with perfecting a technique to use that technique. The basic training is to perfect *yourself*. Traditional training was to train oneself to deal with death. I think really any kind of training teaches you how to die. The Chinese have a saying, the more you sweat in peace the less you bleed in war.

"So it's not that the music is hard, but the discipline is. And the reason for it has gone, we're too materialistic. Nowadays you can play three chords and make a million dollars, so there's no reason to practise. The intention is to reap the most material benefits in the shortest possible time. But all the traditional players are, like, trained in the Samurai mentality. We used to practise ten, 12 hours a day to perfect our art. Which means perfecting yourself."

I'd also like to know, says Katy, to what extent you plan your music. Or does it just arrive at your fingertips?

Ibrahim laughs. "Allah says, you plan and I plan too, and I'm the best of planners.

"We have a book for concerts that we play, but we don't play the same every night. You know Japanese Noh theatre? Noh theatre is, like, the eventual state of bringing the mind, body, soul – bop! – together at one point. The Japanese say Mu Shin, No Mind.

"Now, the playing of what people term jazz comes from what we call in Islam Tariqa, a state of trance. At home we have chants – you say: 'There is no God but He'; say that for five, ten hours, you'll get stoned! I've seen them: one guy thinks he's a rabbit, one guy climbs up the wall—," he hoots with mirth.

"Traditionally, people would call them mad, you know. People in a trance – you could cut them, and there would be no blood. Tariqa! That's where the music comes from and its purpose is to put you in that state, where you are Mu Shin, No Mind. A Japanese swordsman said, 'Under the sword lifted high, there is Hell to make you tremble, but you go ahead anyway if you are No Mind.'

"That's Noh theatre. They can never repeat a movement. That's Sumi painting, too. They don't rub it out and do it again, it's like – ah, ah, ah, finished! Same with the music."

He frowns for a moment, then adds reflectively, "And that's the war that's being fought on this planet. Between the normal people and the crazy ones."

Mind and No Mind, says Katy.

"Right! And the crazy ones are winning it. There's no way you can overcome it. That's what's happening in Iran, Beirut. People with No Mind. Completely *out* of their mind. You must be to drive a truck with 2000lb of explosives into a building.

"It's what happened in Vietnam, too. It's happening all over the world. And there's no way you can fight against that kind of war unless you are prepared to do the same thing. Now, if you are worried about your mortgage, or how you're going to die—," he chuckles softly.

"So, with the music, it's that state of No Mind. You play the music and it takes the audience with you. The music serves as a natural narcotic to drug you, so we can fly into the darker recesses of your soul, where you would not normally dare to go yourself. What did Duke say? 'Come with me to my emerald rock garden, where cellophane trees grow a mile high and the darkness is just a transblucency'."

Ibrahim smiles, his mind on Ellington. "Duke says the blues – you know, people are always asking, what *is* the blues?" He grins. "Man, I read all the books on it. I exhausted the public library and then I said, get me more books! They say, like, 'The blues is a flattened third and a flattened seventh and the blue note is a bended note of despair sung by the people in the cotton fields'." He laughs uproariously. "'Then the blues went up the river to Chicago and Kansas City.' You know how they talk!

"Duke said, 'The blues is the accompaniment to a man and a

woman going steady. And if neither of them wants to sing the blues, the blues just vamps until they are ready'." He guffaws again. "You know, they asked Duke, how would you like to record with John Coltrane? Duke said, 'that would be an *unmitigated gas*'."

Abdullah practically collapses on the floor with laughter. "Duke, man," he gasps. "Oooeee, he was fantastic!"

July 1983/March 1984

CHRIS McGREGOR
An African Way Of Swing

In the clouds a few thousand feet above Chicago, a small aircraft is running into trouble.

"I think we've gone past the airport," says pilot Chris McGregor, pointing to a big blob on the radar screen. "We'd better turn around." He plots a course, then taps a dial on the instrument panel. "Give me a shout when that thing reaches 236." The plane begins to turn.

"Are we high enough?" mutters co-pilot Nick White. I shrug my shoulders.

Suddenly the dials go haywire. The clouds break and we can see the ground rushing up towards us. To my surprise, it appears to be turning cartwheels.

"What's happening?" I ask, alarmed.

The word 'CRASH' flashes before my eyes.

"Oh dear!" McGregor gives a deep, throaty chuckle. "We're dead, that's what's happening."

It's not often I begin an interview by plummeting out of the skies into an early grave, even if it is only on a flight simulator – prize toy in the flat McGregor is, er, crashing in during a brief visit to London – but a cup of tea quickly revives us. Then we're off on a different trip, one that starts half a century ago in South Africa's Transkei province, takes us through Cape Town, Antibes, Zurich and London, where the arrival of McGregor and his fellow Blue Notes (Dudu Pukwana, Mongezi Feza, Johnny Dyani, Louis Moholo) stirred up such ferment in the mid-60s, then whisks us off again around Europe and back to Africa with – hang on to your hat – the wonderful, tumultuous McGregor big band, Brotherhood Of Breath.

The Brotherhood, renowned for their whooping, zonking, free-form swing, have not been seen much in the UK these last few years, but they remain McGregor's chief project and have recently toured in both Europe and Mozambique. Intriguingly, their latest lp *Yes Please* (1981), on the French In And Out label, offers a far more formal, structured music than the raging, raggedy glory of earlier Ogun shots. What, I wondered, had brought about this change?

"There is a direction that's becoming stronger," McGregor says thoughtfully. "I feel a need for simple things, after all the chop of the 70s. So *Yes Please*, that structured thing— I wanted to make it *light*. How can I explain?" He sips his tea, brow furrowed. "The aim was on the *group* happening rather than individuals. And this is an African thing. The music I grew up with in the Transkei is a very communal music, and I have clear memories of the beauty of things directed towards a group. So this development— it's part of the fact that I'm realising I'm an African."

Chris McGregor looks more hippy sage than African. A tall, stocky, cheerful man with humorous eyes and ready smile, his most distinctive features are a long grey beard and even longer grey hair worn in a ponytail that hangs all the way down to his ample waist. But African he is.

He was born in the Transkei nearly 50 years ago, into a Scottish missionary family, and his father taught at the local mission school. He began playing piano at the age of six and first heard jazz on the radio, "Fats Waller, Duke Ellington"; but the predominant influence of his childhood years was the Xhosa tribal music of the Transkei countryside.

"The tribal people, the Red Blanket people, stayed with the old ways," he recalls, "so that music, that way of life, was still going on and it was a very musical culture. People travelling would announce themselves by singing from a hilltop; everyone had their own musical visiting card."

McGregor left the Transkei for college in Cape Town, where he studied European classical music by day and played jazz by night. Though he proved an able student, especially adept at composition, when he left college he became a full-time jazz musician.

"I found I couldn't line myself up behind that Occidental tradition," he says. "I felt it wasn't feeding me, that it wasn't mine. Something in my creativity wasn't being satisfied at all. I didn't realise then what it was, but I know now: I grew up with different stuff."

He spent the next few years playing around the city's clubs, bars and cafés. Cape Town, a large seaport with a local tradition of liberalism, boasted a cosmopolitan culture that was unique in South Africa and, at the beginning of the 60s, jazz thrived. Dollar Brand was making a name for himself, and the hit musical *King Kong*, featuring Miriam Makeba, Hugh Masekela and Kippie Moeketsi, was in full swing. In areas that were not racially zoned, like the edges of the black District Six (later physically torn apart by apartheid legislation), musicians could find plenty of work.

"We'd play every night, rehearse every day. We even had a residency in a curry-house. Regular employment!" McGregor laughs. "Oh boy, whatever happened to that?"

The Blue Notes came together in Cape Town in the early 60s but, as their fame spread, they began to play farther afield. Between 1962 and 1964, when they left South Africa, the band spent nearly all of their time on the road. But there was an ulterior motive.

"We began living on the road as a way of avoiding the restrictions of apartheid," says McGregor. The trick was not to plan your itinerary or book gigs in advance. "We'd just turn up, play a concert and then leave before there was trouble. We discovered that moving was an antidote to apartheid. There's something symbolic in that," he chuckles, "dance, stay on the move, and you'll beat apartheid."

But were there no problems with the Blue Notes being a racially mixed band? I ask. (McGregor was white, the other musicians black.)

He shrugs. "Well, to the extent that we were on the road, it was almost like we were 1000 feet up. We only came down to earth when there was a road-block and then we pretended we were a gang of labourers with a captain. We had some well-rehearsed routines: I became the boss and these were my boys, and we were on our way to fulfil a contract somewhere."

So you never got into serious trouble?

"Only minor scrapes. Especially compared to people I knew who were locked away for 180 days and variously tortured. But usually we were not actually breaking the law."

McGregor's instinct for sidestepping trouble goes back to the time he first became aware of apartheid, at the age of nine or ten, when a group of school friends rounded on him for saying "Good morning" to an elderly black man. "From then on I adopted a kind of invisibility policy. I just wasn't there when things got shitty. I suppose that could fairly well describe how I went through most of my years in South Africa."

He smiles ruefully. "But it's amazing how visible you can get through being invisible."

In fact, it was the Blue Notes' success, and subsequent notoriety, which contributed to their decision to leave South Africa. They were, says McGregor, becoming the focus for a lot of "strange stuff".

"We excited people, and when those armed policemen see a crowd of excited black people, they start fingering their holsters. It was a nervous, trigger-happy atmosphere and I was glad to get out of it."

In 1964 the Blue Notes were invited to play at the Antibes Jazz Festival. They spent the rest of the summer busking around the Côte d'Azur; then, thanks to old friend Dollar Brand, they got a regular gig at Zurich's Afrikaaner Café. After a further 12 months scuffling in Switzerland, they were offered a residency at Ronnie Scott's and so, in 1965, London became their home base. The Blue Notes' Afro-bop, with the volcanic Pukwana sax, Feza's darting trumpet and a truly stormy rhythm section, proved a crucial force in the city's burgeoning New Music scene. But it was a month at Copenhagen's Montmartre Club in 1966 that really turned Chris McGregor around.

The Blue Notes' material had been written by Dudu Pukwana, while McGregor took care of organisational matters: now, with four free weeks, he could concentrate on his own music again, and assimilate the new sounds that were in the air – Cecil Taylor, Albert Ayler, Don Cherry.

Though a willing talker, Chris McGregor gets a little uneasy when I ask him to explain the changes he was going through at that time.

"Talking about these things assumes quite a lot of consciousness about what you're doing and I'm not the kind of person who conceptualises all that much. Things grow inside you and, er— you don't really know, you don't make conscious choices: you're a player and things creep into your playing. You just get a feeling for areas you want to explore."

Which were? I press him.

He frowns. "It was to do with African polyrhythms. I started hearing the possibilities of things happening on a lot of different levels rhythmically. There was a wheel turning then, things flowing together in a way they no longer seem to be. Not that I want to raise any barriers, er—" he pauses. "Perhaps it would be easier if I said why I'm not that much associated now with what you'd call free jazz."

I nod.

"It's—," he pauses again, then bursts out laughing. "Ah, I don't know what I'm gonna say now! I think it's that African thing again. Since that time I feel much more African, I really have to see it from an African viewpoint. And in African music there's a lot of polyrhythmic structure that's quite a lot more advanced than most of what you find in the West." Perplexed, he tugs at his beard, then shrugs. "I don't know how to say it any better."

Although the Blue Notes galvanised the British jazz scene, it was McGregor's 1970 big band Brotherhood Of Breath who really shook the foundations, with their gleeful and exuberant approach to swing. Their music, says McGregor, was a conscious extension of the tradition epitomised by his idol, Duke Ellington.

"I'm an absolute nut for big bands. I love the colours and the energy flow of big groups. I've always been ultra-attracted by that organisation and putting-together capacity that was so uniquely Duke's. I love playing, arranging, composing – the lot!"

In the Brotherhood, Blue Notes, plus some South African expatriates, plus the more adventurous young British players, jostled together cheek by jowl, the band's personnel reading like a Who's Who of 70s' Brit Jazz: Harry Beckett, Marc Charig, Nick Evans, Radu Malfatti, Harry Miller, Evan Parker, John Surman. Et cetera. Their lps – two for RCA, two for Ogun – present a fierce, potent mix of African polyrhythms, American swing and European free-form that could reach truly Brothering heights. Together with the intergalactic forays of the Sun Ra Arkestra, they swept the big-band tradition into territories barely dreamed of before, let alone charted.

But, as the African elements in McGregor's music come to the fore – like the 'lightness', the structures, of *Yes Please* – it seems there is now less room for improvisation. Is that the case?

"Ha," his eyes gleam, "that *is* something to talk about. In the West people talk about jazz as if improvisation is the cardinal thing, as if jazz *equals* improvisation. But for me that begs too many questions. I have this strong imaginative reference to African village music, and the thing I know about that music is that it has a strong centre. It builds up, a lot of people do things together that they *know*. What is that? It's not a composition but it's in the culture of the people – they know the moves. Yet it's not all prearranged, you have people interpreting the moves in their own way, though those individual flights will always come clearly from the feeling of the moves that have been established.

"So the key isn't improvisation, yet the music is very *alive* – there's such a mix of old and new, solo and group. It's very fluid, dynamic, creative, and in my music I'm looking for something like that. So, in African music, improvisation isn't meaningful *in essence*. Creativity is, but that's something else. That's what Brotherhood Of Breath is about, creating in groups. And I find I can accept the orthodox disciplines of jazz more easily now, because we no longer have those community traditions but we still need that community feeling, and if it means a certain amount of structuring to create, like, a kind of instant tradition, instant reference points, then that's OK – as long as the structures don't become strictures."

Since Chris McGregor went to live in the French countryside several years ago, Britain has seen less of Brotherhood Of Breath. But, despite the economic and logistic problems of running the band, and despite a separate solo career (check out Ogun's *In His Good Time* and the two volumes of *Piano Song* on Musica), the Brotherhood remains McGregor's most cherished project: his ideal is to have the band on the road full-time, *à la* Duke. "Not as an institution," he insists, "but as a community. We'll get there too, I'm sure."

Meanwhile he's touting tapes of recent Paris concerts around the record companies; and the band's tour of Mozambique last year has inspired a new work, with singers and dancers, which he hopes to complete by the summer. The Brotherhood are still breathing strong.

As the afternoon ticks by, our talk spins on and on. We cover some heavy topics there's no room to report on here: politics, philosophy, Sisterhood Of Spit! But let's just squeeze in a bit of that $64,000 question – music's role in solving the world's problems. It is, asserts McGregor, "absolutely crucial. Music orients minds and spirits. I really don't think there's anything more important you can do."

Doesn't that responsibility impinge on your creativity? I ask

"Ah, no, you can't do anything except try to remain true to what's pushing you," he declares. "You *can* direct your inspiration to a certain extent but it's very little. I think we all have guardian angels who direct us— yeah, really!" – he sees the look of disbelief cross my face – "Who direct human thoughts, aspirations, orientations. And for musicians it's important to stay next to the one who's telling you. So you can't really direct it: except at great risk. If you try, you dry up. Or you find yourself just going through the motions, and that's the worst pain ever. That's like— when people say they'd rather die, I believe them. It's like denying the well-springs of your being."

Hmm? Guardian angels? But I'm half-persuaded by the passion of McGregor's belief. He frowns, still thinking it through.

"I know there's a problem in that some people who are used to seeing things in a very, er, distinct way may find it hard to know what it is that's pushing them. I don't quite know what to say about that." He absently rolls a a strand of beard between thumb and forefinger. "I guess you have to approach it with your instincts, just grab hold of whatever's coming and follow it through."

He looks up and laughs. "Really, that's all. *That* is a musician's work. It's a great life, too. I wouldn't edit my story at all. When I think back there's nothing I regret, nothing that seems to me to have been wrong or off-key.

"You have to be 50 years old to realise, though," he chuckles deeply. "That's maybe one thing there *is* to regret, that we get too soon old and too late smart."

A perfect sign-off line, from the master of structure.

September 1984

BILLIE HOLIDAY

A review of
The Lady And The Legend
(Rhapsody RHA 6025/6/7)
Recorded: 1949-1958

Feminist film criticism has focused attention on how cinema is "constructed according to the unconscious of patriarchy", which means that women in film do not "function as signifiers for a signified (a real woman)" but that "signifier and signified have been elided into a sign that represents something in the male unconscious".[1]

Apart from Robyn Archer's *A Star Is Torn* show, I don't know of any equivalent feminist analysis of music, but the power nexus here must work in a similar way. On the most obvious level, male critics tend to both see women performers in terms of sexuality and as often (mis)construe that sexuality in their own minds as see what – if anything – is really there. Take the remark on a recent lp sleevenote that Julie London's voice came "decked out in a sheer black négligée": here the male critic doesn't just make the voice into a sex object, he further turns it into a fetishistic object of male fantasy.

I mention all this because I'm trying to find a way of understanding my unease about some of Billie Holiday's later recordings. This unease centres around what Alice Walker calls those "embarrassing anything-for-a-man songs" – songs, like 'My Man', 'Don't Explain', 'You're My Thrill', that comprised the greater part of her repertoire in later years. In these songs women's dependence on men is portrayed in extreme and absolute terms; even, in 'My Man' and 'T'Ain't Nobody's Business', to the extent of accepting and condoning male violence. What bothers me is a) why did Billie Holiday sing these songs? and b) why were they popular, what did people *hear* in them (other than the art of the singer)?

The glib answer is that these songs told the truth. Well, it's a fact that Billie Holiday *was* cruelly treated by many men; and this tragic confluence of life and art does colour these songs with a quality that, for me, is harsher and more unsettling than simple poignancy.

But whatever truth these songs tell is surely more than one of personal circumstance: something else they make manifest is women's powerlessness in a male society. This is an aspect of the music which I suspect is heard differently (consciously or unconsciously) by men and women – ie, to generalise, with satisfaction, even perverse pleasure, by the former, with bitter recognition by the latter. It may be fanciful to hear a sub-text of protest in these songs, but in addition to their surface statement of female submissiveness they also make it clear that a lot of men are shits and that domestic male violence is pretty much an everyday affair. (In the track 'My Man' the contrast between romantic utterance and real life is so stark as to verge on the bleakly parodic: *"he beats me too— oh, my man I love him so".*)

A further paradox is that Billie Holiday expresses this powerlessness through the one source of power available to her – the power of her art. There's a sentimental view which sees her art as shaped and fed by the tragedies of her life. In fact, the reverse is true. It's not just that her artistry is unmistakable from her earliest recordings, but that her art was, crucially, the one area of her life where she had control, her weapon in the struggle for survival. This is both true literally (it was how she made her living) and metaphorically, in that it was through her art, her specific qualities as a great singer, that she gave voice to and shaped the vicissitudes of her life. This may be why she sang those songs, as a form of symbolic control, as way of giving her everyday hassles an *authenticity* that could be heard by all. One thing I am sure of, we still have a lot to hear in Billie Holiday's music.

To business. These three albums are compiled from tv, radio and live recordings from the last ten years of her life and were originally available on ESP. Quality, of sound and performance, is variable but generally better than fair. The highlights here, like the Storyville tracks, the 1957 'Fine And Mellow', have been widely available for years; and, in fact, an almost identical three-lp series on Happy Bird – *Tenderly, All Of Me, Porgy* – has just been released in the UK.

Both the Rhapsody and Happy Bird sets share faults that are common to many Billie Holiday compilations: meagre and banal sleeve-notes (excepting *Tenderly*), incomplete discographical data and tacky covers. The Rhapsody set scores on two counts: it has 40 tracks to Happy Bird's 39 (though to complicate matters Rhapsody has six not on Happy Bird, Happy Bird five not on Rhapsody) and it dates them all – something which the *All Of Me* lp mysteriously fails to do: even stranger, the track described as 'All Of Me' on that album turns out to be another version of 'My Man'.

Such carelessness implies a disrespect for the artist that is typical of capitalist record companies. These lps rely on selling Billie Holiday as a myth – the Great Jazz Victim – a ploy which, like pornography, basically glamorises a woman's pain. (Curiously, the cover photo on the Happy Bird lps makes her look as if she's just been hit.) But Billie Holiday did not epitomise suffering, she *articulated* it; and that she did so honestly was part of her strength. To refer incessantly to her vulnerability and sensitivity, to see her purely as a victim, is almost to blame *her* for her tragically early death. This is a mystification which only distracts attention from her real killers: sexism, racism and, at the end, in Mal Waldron's bitter phrase, "an overdose of police".

published November 1984

1. Quotes from E. Ann Kaplan's 'Is The Gaze Male?' in *Desire*: *The Politics Of Sexuality* – eds. Snitow, Stansell and Thompson (London: Virago, 1984).

MIKE WESTBROOK
Sweet Thunder

The night Mama Chicago hits town, the air is filled with fire and sweat. In the Seven Dials, blood slides down the wall. You're *there*, in slaughter-house, in clip-joint, as cattle scream and the Windy City boogies on down against Depression. The rain from Lake Michigan stings your face; the ghost of Al Capone leans on the bar, machine-gun still smoking.

The Brass Band blast out the beat, swing it through Duke and Cab and Jelly Roll. Then it's a march or a sour, late-night blues. Phil Minton moooaaans, Chris Biscoe blows a tear-stained solo. Kate Westbrook cackles of *"golden guys and dolls"*, all gone to dust.

In the shadows a figure looms. The Boss. He grunts through a tuba, slaps down piano keys. His elbows poke through frayed shirtsleeves. Huh? I second-take. Times are *that* tough? Then the Creole rhythms catch afire, the mind dances, the spirits fly.

I step into the night, dazed, happy, head full of fantasy. *"Darkness falls from smoky air / The future is already here."* A long black limousine pulls up beside me, the door swings open.

"Get in," growls a voice. "Big Mike wants to see ya!"

The day I meet Mike Westbrook he has just returned from Sicily, where he and his co-worker/wife Kate have been researching a new music-theatre piece based on D.H. Lawrence's poem 'The Ass'. 1985 is a big year for Westbrook. 'The Ass', scheduled for Nottingham's Lawrence festival in September, will be preceded by two other British premières of new Westbrook material. In May, *On Duke's Birthday* – his orchestral tribute to Ellington – plays at a central London venue, and in June the

Queen Elizabeth Hall will stage his *Westbrook-Rossini*, a composition for seven-piece brass band based on the opera *William Tell*.

Given the scope of Westbrook's previous work, Ellington and Lawrence are not unexpected reference points. But Rossini?

It all began, he says, when the Westbrooks were invited to play at a Lausanne street festival dedicated to William Tell. Kate – a keen opera fan – suggested using the Rossini and Mike, dubious at first, became fascinated by both the music and the composer's life-story. His *modus operandi* particularly appealed.

"All his operas were written in about ten days, just before the deadlines. He was always working under pressure – last-minute rehearsals, chaos, riots on the first night, people throwing things. Not at all one's picture of the classical opera – more like a jazz gig, really!"

It's Mike Westbrook's talent for nosing out new directions, unlikely links, that has made him the leading British jazz figure of his time. Though inspired by the great tradition of black composers such as Ellington and Mingus, Westbrook has also drawn on an Old World culture of folk songs, poetry, cabaret and hymns, so forging in his music a unique marriage of African, American and European sensibilities. In particular, from big-band projects like *Metropolis* and *Citadel/Room 315* to his settings of William Blake's poetry and his epic musical canvas *The Cortege*, Westbrook has shown himself to be a composer of extraordinary flair and vision. It's no surprise to hear that, fired by *William Tell*, Westbrook is toying with the idea of doing an opera himself.

"It is the ultimate performance art," he enthuses. "It has everything – story, poetry, music, spectacle, acting. You have to have a big vision to take it all in."

That's exactly what Mike Westbrook's got. But in person I find it partly hidden behind a very English sense of decorum. A large, friendly man whose slightly gauche air is rather disarming (and deceptive), his conversation reveals both a native reserve (Religious beliefs, Mike? "Well—er," twiddles fingers, shifts uneasily, looks stern, "I, er, don't think this is really the time or place—") and, pulling against it, a desire to explain his music with the same painstaking thoroughness that goes into its making. Now more than ever, it seems.

"Yes, I find writing's become slower, much more difficult," he frowns. "I think as you get older you become more aware of all the possibilities. Also I've become more interested in craftsmanship, in the architecture of the music, and that discipline is hard. I can't leave things out, for example. My things are often accused of being too long, and, certainly, when you look at Ellington's three-minute masterpieces, I don't know how he did it.

"I can't do *anything* three minutes long," self-deprecating chuckle, shake of head. "That economy is something we've lost."

Mike Westbrook was a late developer in jazz. Born in High Wycombe in 1936, he grew up in Torquay, then spent seven years sampling accountancy, National Service, geography and art school before he realised music was his first love. He started his first band in Plymouth in 1958 and was soon joined by baritonist John Surman, then a 16-year-old schoolboy. (One possible legacy of this early encounter is that nearly every Westbrook band since has featured baritone.) In 1962 they both moved to London, where Westbrook led numerous bands, large and small, and played regularly at the Old Place and the Little Theatre Club, as well as holding down a day job as an art teacher. In 1968 his band made their international début at the Montreux Festival.

His first records – *Celebration* (1967), *Release* (1968), *Marching Song* (1969 – all Deram) – were large-scale, big-band works, which showed Westbrook rapidly expanding his modern jazz base to include blues, rock & roll, brass bands, Lionel Hampton and 'The Girl From Ipanema' in glorious profusion. Two unrecorded pieces, 'Earthrise', and the seven-and-a-half hour 'Copan/Backing Track', were early examples of Westbrook's interest in multimedia projects, particularly music-theatre, and employed lightshows, costume, film and slides. "This body of work," wrote Ian Carr in 1973, "was responsible for the emancipation of British jazz from American slavery."[1]

Metropolis (RCA, 1971) was the culmination of this first big-band phase, and, with its use of a double rhythm section and electric guitars, also paved the way for Westbrook's brief fling with rock music in his group Solid Gold Cadillac. He'd been attracted by rock's "power and strength", by its focus on the song form, but when the records didn't sell, his RCA contract "fizzled out" and the band soon followed suit. Westbrook later returned to RCA for a one-off, the *Citadel/Room 315* big-band project in 1975, but, in the meantime, his attention had turned to the format which, along with the big band, has proved the most durable of his concerns: the Brass Band.

Formed in 1973 with old Torquay crony Phil Minton, Westbrook found the Brass Band an ideal vehicle for his interests in popular song and theatre. It was, he says, a new start; a deliberate attempt to "be more accessible, to play to people in different situations". For the next few years, the Brass Band forsook the usual music circuits and played at fringe theatre events, street festivals, factories, schools, hospitals. Audiences enthused but costs were prohibitive.

"We were really scuffling," he recalls. "I can't tell you. No money at all, no record contract, we were nowhere."

At this point, Kate Barnard (later Westbrook), who had joined the band soon after its inception on vocals, tenor horn and piccolo, sat down with a telephone directory and rang every record company in London.

"We made appointments with all the A & R men, took them our little cassettes of Brass Band music," Westbrook says grimly. "Some were too busy to see us, some didn't even turn up. We saw, like, the whole underbelly of the music business. Some of those guys were absolute shits."

Luckily, Transatlantic were keen to help and offered a deal whereby Westbrook was paid a regular monthly sum. It was, he says, the only time in his entire musical career that he has had real financial security. Alas, within months, the company was taken over and Westbrook's deal fell through. But a turning point of sorts had been reached: the Brass Band made their first lp (*For The Record*, 1976) and Westbrook met Laurence Aston, who later left Transatlantic and released several Westbrook records on his own label, Original Records. He also became the Westbrooks' manager.

Such vicissitudes are not untypical of a British jazz scene which is consistently undervalued by Arts Council snobbery and government philistinism, but Westbrook – as a composer and brass-band leader – is an anomaly even within the jazz culture.

Does he ever feel like an outsider?

"Yes. I find it all very frustrating. Kate and I, when we start to think about where we fit in, even on the jazz scene, which is surely where we belong, we both feel very isolated. And the Arts Council, Radio

Three – they have such a constricted view of music.

"But," he adds, "one can't help being aware that jazz music is not very widely accepted in this country. It's run up against brick walls."

Such as?

"Well, the emphasis on commercial music. You seem like a romantic fool if you don't do things for money." He shrugs helplessly. "There's a kind of cynicism, perhaps it's the Thatcher ethic, which has crept into all areas of life. Idealism, sincerity, playing the music you *believe* in, that's all regarded as old-fashioned. It's sell, sell, sell – it runs right through the cultural establishment, as well as the pop business, and I don't think that jazz fits into that scheme.

"Still," he reckons, "jazz has a fundamental strength. The people who do believe in it, believe passionately. Young musicians are still coming up and committing themselves to the music. OK, all those prosaic things like paying the rent, God knows they are problems, but in bigger terms, even if we in jazz are struggling, it's a noble struggle. We have to stick to our guns."

Of the seven albums Westbrook made between 1976 and 1981, five were by the Brass Band. Truly, a case of where there's Mike, there's brass! *For The Record*, *Goose Sauce* (1978) and the live *Paris Album* (1981) offer selections from the band's repertoire; *Mama Chicago* (1979), a jazz cabaret based on the life of Al Capone, and *The Westbrook Blake* (1980) are more programmatic.

For me, Westbrook's *Blake* is a highlight of his career. His settings of Blake's great radical and visionary poems were originally written in 1971 for Adrian Mitchell's play *Tyger*, but he later adapted them for the Brass Band and they became a staple part of the repertoire. This honing process paid rich dividends: *The Westbrook Blake* is among the most potent and stirring of modern jazz albums. Superbly performed by the band – horns and voices relishing the emotion with visceral intensity – Westbrook's music perfectly catches Blake's feeling, from the mystical joy of 'I See Thy Form' to the bitter anguish of 'London Song'. Westbrook's comment that "there's something in Blake that's close to the spirituality of Coltrane" perhaps explains why the saxophonists here (Chris Biscoe, Alan Wakeman) blow with such blood-curdling passion. And the finale – Phil Minton singing 'Let The

Slave', Westbrook declaiming 'The Price Of Experience' – meets Blake's vision of political freedom, his mighty plea on behalf of the wretched of the earth, with a fervour and commitment that swell the heart.

Then there's the bleak anger of 'Holy Thursday', one of several songs here with an uncanny relevance to Thatcher's Britain: *"Is this a holy thing to see/In a rich and fruitful land/Babes reduc'd to misery/Fed with a cold and usurous hand?"*

"It's a cry of tremendous compassion," agrees Westbrook. "The world hasn't changed that much since Blake's time. Even London is much the same as 'London Song'. I think Blake got to the heart of the human situation."

He adds that he and Kate also recorded Blake's 'The Human Abstract' as a single for CND. So where does Westbrook see himself politically? Is he a socialist?

"Oh yes, of course," he says, surprised. "I've never been able to imagine how any reasonably intelligent person could be anything else. And one's experience as a musician confirms it. I think jazz *is* a socialist music; it has to be – because of its very nature, its origins, the whole image of society which is contained in the activity of playing jazz."

Hang on, how do you as *composer* fit into this egalitarian vision? Aren't you in charge?

"It has to be the kind of vision of society or collective activity where people contribute what they're best at, not one where they have to deny part of themselves to fit in. It does work in jazz groups. When you're onstage, there's an incredible equality between all the performers, everyone is mutually dependent. I think jazz is a much more collective activity than people acknowledge."

Yet, apart from a handful of songs about war and poverty, your own work rarely addresses specific political issues: how come?

He ponders. "Well, when it happens, it's wonderful. But I don't think it's something one can aim for as a thing in itself. Propagandist music makes things very simplistic, musically and politically, whereas in fact things are much more complex, and I think the artist must try to use the finest language that he's capable of – not to be obscure, but he mustn't be dishonest or go against his nature.

"Basically, I believe one *must* have artistic integrity, artistic freedom, because that's what gives you the determination to carry on."

In recent years, Westbrook's major project has been *The Cortege*, an epic, three-hour work for voices and 16-piece jazz orchestra. First performed at Bracknell in 1979, Westbrook made substantial revisions before it was recorded for Original in 1982.

The Cortege reflects on no less a theme than "the cycle Life/Death/Life" and Westbrook cites two images as central to the work. The first, that of a horseman riding to his death, comes from Lorca's poem *Cancion De Jinete*, here given a solemn setting on 'Cordoba'. The second, that of a New Orleans funeral march, evokes an early black musical tradition – the parade that begins in grief and ends in elation.

Rather a sombre framework, I remark.

"The real facts of our existence are pretty sombre," Westbrook shrugs. "There are times when one wants to do simple, immediate things and that's fine, and other times when you want to do something bigger, to try and crack some of the big problems of existence, and *The Cortege* is like that."

The idea grew out of the Westbrooks' travels around Europe, was fed by such diverse influences as Goya's etchings and Stravinsky's *The Soldier's Tale*, and gradually took shape as a huge musical procession of Westbrookalia: texts from Rimbaud, Blake, Lorca, folk songs from Sweden, taut chamber sections, rock guitar solos, brass-band marches, big-band swing. "It encompassed everything I knew in 1979," he grins, "probably still does."

If the overall mood is necessarily dark, there is satire, elegy and a rumbustious drinking song to lighten the way. Plus a stream of fine solos, notably Phil Todd's clarinet, Lindsay Cooper's sopranino and Phil Minton's voice, which can ride the swell of Blake, yet wrap itself in the eeriest of rustic tones for a garish 'Lady Howerd's Coach'. But *The Cortege* is chiefly an ensemble work, a prime example of Westbrook's developing interest in musical "architecture". Much of the music, he says, grew out of a nine-note sequence which forms the bass line of 'Cordoba', the first section he wrote.

"I've always been interested in developing my own sense of harmony, and working on the structure of *The Cortege* involved me in a lot of experimentation, a lot of mathematics, drawings. I was trying to evolve— I lack the exact terminology, but I suppose it was a scheme of tonality. That nine-note sequence fascinated me and I began to form a pattern, a matrix, and explore the ramifications of that."

The number three, says Westbrook, became a vital component of *The Cortege*, both thematically (the Life/Death/Life cycle) and musically, where it formed "the basis for rhythmic, melodic and harmonic patterns". In particular, in its evocation of the Holy Trinity, it reflected the Christian elements of the work.

"Broadly, yes, Kate and I would describe ourselves as Christians," he says when pressed, though I suspect he's more at ease with Blake's visionary iconoclasm than with any particular set of church dogma. Like his politics, his religious beliefs are rarely explicit in his music, and even in the case of 'Kyrie', the one specifically Christian reference in *The Cortege*, Westbrook's programme notes stress that it is "a simple universal framework of spiritual communion". Its form, he also points out, is "equivalent to the most fundamental musical form in jazz, itself wrung from the cries of suffering humanity – the 12-bar blues".[2]

Talk of *The Cortege* leads us inevitably to the art of composition itself. In 1983 Westbrook wrote: "Though I started, musically, from a fairly abstract basis, the songs, say, in French and Spanish, took on the character of French and Spanish music, without any effort on my part to make them do so."

I express scepticism about this and push him: surely you had some prior idea of the musical idioms you would use?

"No— er, it's very personal, really, how one works. I, er—," he stops, looking rather harassed. "I don't ever analyse my approach— but, well, the last thing I think about is what idiom the music should go in. If it's for lyrics, I go to the words, and if there are no words, there's a feeling I'm trying to get into, give a shape to— But I have no preconceptions, no barriers: I don't push things in a particular direction, but if I find them going that way I don't try to stop them. So if it turns out like a folk song, or a bit like Ellington, say, that doesn't matter as long as it *works*."

He reflects a moment, then declares: "The only problem ever is expressing what you want to express, and the only criterion is that it doesn't sound boring."

There is so much more to the Westbrook canon that I lack the space to cover: albums like *Love/Dream And Variations* (1976), *Piano* (1977), *A Little Westbrook Music* (1983) and a wealth of unrecorded material, from tv and film scores to jazz cabaret and music-theatre pieces like 'Bartlemy Fair', 'Bien Sur!' and 'Hotel Amigo'. There is also his background in painting to be explored, with particular reference to the strong visual element in Westbrook's composition, from the influence of Goya on *The Cortege* to his visit to Sicily for *The Ass*. ("Oh yes, landscape can be an inspiration.") In 1973 Westbrook spoke of his music as "sound images", now he says he's more interested in its "architecture" than in "just a sequence of images": a change, but the analogy is still to the graphic.

Most vital of all, there is the influence of his wife Kate, which he describes as "paramount". Her songwriting skills, her knowledge of painting, poetry, opera, theatre, have both spurred Westbrook's own interests and led his writing into new areas. Much of this is, I think, evident on the records. But there is more, too.

"Our relationship has been a major factor in us being able to keep up the struggle, as it were, because there have been times of darkest despair, not so long ago really, and having Kate there, someone else believing in the music, gave me the strength to carry on."

One thing I should mention in a little detail is the latest Westbrook lp, *On Duke's Birthday* (Hat Art). Originally part of a longer work, *After Smith's Hotel*, Westbrook revised and added to existing material and came up with a new, separate piece. His love of Ellington goes back to his teenage years, when his father gave him an lp of Duke's 1940s orchestra. "I've been listening to him so long now," he says, "he's in my bloodstream"; and *On Duke's Birthday* includes a couple of sly Ducal touches – wah-wah trombone, high trumpet – as a mark of respect. But it isn't, Westbrook insists, a copy or imitation of the master: "I don't have the technical ability to do that."

It is, though, his tightest piece of composition to date.

"I tried to create a harmonic language, to inter-relate the sections, interlace things harmonically and melodically, so there are cross-references holding it all together. It's quite rigidly structured: all the solos are written into the arrangements, for example, rather than open-ended."

A flawless, polished record, *On Duke's Birthday* reflects the "new confidence" Westbrook says he has found in his writing. Ellington's compliment to English culture on the Shakespeare-inspired *Such Sweet Thunder* has been amply repaid.

To end our conversation, I remind Westbrook of something he said to Ian Carr in 1973. "What I'm after is some kind of spiritual thing. This is a restless quest." Is that still true?

He looks embarrassed. "Er— I expect I'll get in an awful muddle if I talk about it, but, yes, there is a quest, a very deep search for— truth, I suppose. The myriad techniques of music are all ways of approaching it, though it's something you endlessly circle around, never really getting very near it, because we're very imperfect.

"But through music, all the arts, I think one can get into that dimension. And it seems to me that the improviser taking a tune and improvising on it is a good symbol of that process. To take something known – and then the great improvisers have this enormous gift of going beyond that, to where another world can open out to you.

"Blake talked about imagination, that's the technique you use, but the goal is building this vision, this Jerusalem. That's what it's all about in the end."

Mike Westbrook is in his 50th year of building Jerusalem. His music, wrote Ian Carr, "has enlarged the consciousness, receptiveness and potential of British musicians".

Sweet thunder, indeed! Or, as Willy Blake had it, *a blessing on every blast.*

January 1985

1. Ian Carr, *Music Outside* (London: Latimer, 1973).
2. Mike Westbrook, *The Cortege – An Introduction* (London: Original Music, 1983).

NORMA WINSTONE
The Singing Is The Song

Norma Winstone looks vaguely puzzled. "Sometimes I find I'm making a sound I haven't noticed myself making before." She shrugs. "It sounds as if I'm talking about someone else. It's rather like that when I'm singing, as if it's coming from somewhere else, as if it's somebody else who's doing it."

Two Norma Winstones? Well, I can count at least three: the Radio Two Norma Winstone, the Azimuth Norma Winstone and the Drill Hall Norma Winstone.

The Radio Two NW and the Azimuth NW are both well known and virtually antipodean in style: the former sings standards with a BBC big band, the latter improvises wordless vocals on ECM albums with John Taylor and Kenny Wheeler. But it's the Drill Hall Norma Winstone who's my favourite, and that's where my story begins.

I first heard Norma Winstone sing in 1982, at Britain's first festival of women's jazz, which was held in London's Drill Hall. Partnered superbly by John Taylor (Mr Winstone) on piano, she gave an astonishingly bravura performance of vocal power, singing and scatting with a cool intensity that matched feeling with technical finesse. The highlights were her epic readings of 'I'll Remember April' and 'Joy Spring', both featuring magnificent scat interludes, while a brief, heartstopping 'Hi Lili, Hi Lo' and the graceful ballad 'Café' (her lyrics, Egberto Gismonti's tune) came close behind.

The next day I rushed out to buy all the Norma Winstone albums I could find – and hit a snag. There weren't any. The three Azimuth albums were no longer available, and her one solo record, *Edge Of Time*, had long been deleted, as had the many British jazz albums of the late

60s/early 70s on which she sang. As far as the record industry was concerned, Norma Winstone might never have existed.

Three years later, the situation is only marginally better. The Azimuth albums are back in the shops and Winstone is planning to put out a duo album with John Taylor, which will hopefully include much of her Drill Hall material. But the earlier work of a singer who, with Maggie Nicols, Pepi Lemer and Julie Tippetts, pioneered freeform vocals in Britain, remains, sadly, a collector's item.

Norma Winstone began to sing professionally in the early 60s, working with dance bands in her local Dagenham haunts. But, disliking that kind of singing, she packed it in for a couple of years and listened to a lot of modern jazz. Miles Davis and John Coltrane inspired her comeback to music.

"I wanted to incorporate that instrumental freedom in a vocal way. It's what I've been doing all the time, trying to work towards that. To begin with I stuck with words, but I messed about with the tune – some people said a bit too much! The first wordless vocals I did were in 1968, I think, with Michael Garrick."

In an innovatory move, Winstone joined Garrick's group as a frontline *instrumentalist*, eventually replacing saxophonist Jim Philip. The first Garrick lp to feature Winstone was *The Heart Is A Lotus* (Argo, 1970) but her recording début had come the previous year when she guested on one of the great lost albums of British jazz, Joe Harriott's and Amancio D'Silva's lovely *Hum Dono* (Columbia, 1969). Mixing wordless vocals with lyrics, Winstone recorded more albums with Garrick, worked for a year with Mike Westbrook and turned up on projects by John Taylor, Keith Tippett, Kenny Wheeler, SME and others. Her own lp *Edge Of Time* (Argo, 1972) offered a resumé of her skills, ranging across the big-band turbulence of John Surman's 'Erebus' to the calmer, pastoral moods of her collaborations with John Taylor.

But why only the one record under her own name?

"I couldn't find anyone who was interested in recording what I was doing then," she recalls with a gentle sigh. "I suppose it was a question of drive too. I just stayed with the groups I was working with, so if they did a record I did a record. But I think I wasn't really sure for a long time what I wanted to do as a soloist. Perhaps it was due to a lack of confidence."

This reminds me of several quotes in Kitty Grimes' *Jazz Voices* where Winstone talks about stage fright.[1] She says that for many years she was too nervous even to announce the titles of her songs.

"Yes, I couldn't speak. I was terribly frightened. I used to come out in big red blotches too, all over my shoulders and neck. You feel so out of control, things flashing past at 100mph. Your heart beats faster, your voice trembles."

Are there no techniques to help control nerves?

"Try to breathe deeply. It's about all you can do. You just have to keep being nervous, going through it, like a baptism of fire. Gradually you find ways of dealing with it."

Do you still feel stage fright now?

"Yes. Not always. But you don't know when it'll happen. I suppose I can cope with it better now – but it doesn't feel like it from the inside."

After *Edge Of Time* came a hiatus. Winstone tried to run a quintet for a while, but work was scarce and it proved too difficult to keep the group together. For the next few years, she says, her "creative instincts" were directed to bringing up her two children, and when she felt ready to return to full-time singing, she found British jazz was still in the doldrums.

She and John Taylor prepared a demo tape and, "in desperation, really", Taylor took it to Germany. Luckily, ECM boss Manfred Eicher liked one of the pieces – a synthesizer and voice sequence they'd tacked on "as an afterthought" – and suggested adding a flugelhorn. Taylor and Winstone called up their old friend Kenny Wheeler – and Azimuth was born.

"It was," sums up Winstone, "all pretty haphazard."

The Azimuth albums – *Azimuth* (1977), *The Touchstone* (1978) and *Départ* (1980, with guitarist Ralph Towner) – are full of the fine playing you'd expect from three outstanding musicians; but they present a rather rarified style of jazz – delicate, freefall improvisations around Taylor's cool, spacious compositions. The feel is perhaps more reminiscent of modern composers such as Delius and Peter Warnock than of the African-American jazz tradition.

For Winstone the ECM recordings marked a curious turning point. It was the first time she had liked the sound of her voice.

"For a long time I was so interested in improvising I tended to ignore the *sound* I made, which I think was a mistake. Most times when I listened to playbacks, I didn't really like my voice. But the ECM recordings convinced me I could actually make a pleasant sound and that influenced the way I sang. I've thought a lot more about my sound since then."

Winstone's improvisations are strikingly *musical*; by which I mean she foregoes the battery of vocal effects used by most other free singers. There's none of Maggie Nicols' joking or surreal hiccups, none of Phil Minton's anguished yelps and howls; just clearly formed notes that ring out in a remarkably pure tone.

"It's been called a choirboy's voice," she laughs. "It's a kind of voice that seems to blend well with instruments, so it's suited to making *textures*."

Azimuth blend textures exceptionally well. But that's only one facet of Winstone's talent: her ability to interpret and scat within the song format has gone unrecorded for far too long. That's why she's keen to do the duo lp with John Taylor. It will, she says, be "a wordy sort of album – it's time to do something with words".

I ask if she adopts different approaches for singing with and without words.

"No, it's the same technique you're using. It's still singing."

How about differences in emotional content? Presumably, with lyrics the emotion is more specific?

"Well, you can create a mood without a story," she ponders. "But yes, with lyrics there is usually a specific mood. Without words the music can go in different directions perhaps; there's more freedom."

When you sing without lyrics, do you still try to instil emotion in the music or is your focus more abstract, more technical?

"I don't really think about the technical side, at least no more without words than with. I always want it to be an emotional experience. For me, singing is very emotional anyway. Perhaps words draw people in more easily, though I feel I'm like an actress when I sing words. You can be more yourself without them."

So improvising is still the biggest thrill?

"Yes, it stretches you. It's living dangerously, really, that's what I like about it. I couldn't bear to sing and know every time what was going to come out. But sometimes I do like to take a song and do it in a particular way, to make something that's technically difficult sound good. That's a challenge, too."

She smiles apologetically. "Basically, I just like singing."

January 1985

1. Kitty Grimes, *Jazz Voices* (London: Quartet, 1983).

MAX ROACH
Cymbals Of Change

The great drummer looks at me askance. What is it? All I did was wonder aloud why so many bebop musicians had wrecked their lives through drug abuse.

"You know how hard drugs came into America?" He asks.

I shake my head. He leans forward, savouring the role of teacher.

"Cocaine was first introduced into the black community during slavery. The slave owners discovered that cocaine cut the appetite and gave people high energy, so they brought it up from South America to increase the productivity of the African slaves.

"That's how it started, then it infused the rest of the black community. And when they brought the Chinese labourers in to build the Atlantic-Pacific railroad in the 1800s, that's when opium was introduced into the US – again, to boost the workers' productivity. It was all to do with economics."

He leans back in his chair, smiling at the surprise on my face. I should have expected a history lesson from this man; Max Roach is not only the greatest drummer in the history of jazz, a veteran of the bebop revolution, he's also one of the sharpest political brains in the business.

"The artists got involved for other reasons, to escape," he adds quietly. "But the use of drugs among artists has been very small compared to their economic uses. Now they're like a disease all over the country. Hard drugs are rampant everywhere – in the business world!

"I read an article recently about the computer industry; there's a city in California where all the personal computer firms are based, and they have a big thing about cocaine there, because the competition is so fierce. It's used for the same reasons – increasing productivity, just like they did with the slaves."

He chuckles at the irony. Karma moves in mysterious ways.

Do you think, I ask, that the US government made heroin available to defuse the post-war black political unrest for which bebop was a catalyst?

"No—well," he pauses, "I'm sure there was a political dimenison. It's part of the whole oppressive attitude of the ruling class; they use drugs to suppress people, keep them from thinking in their never-never land.

"But I don't think the government really feared— even with the whole Civil Rights upheaval in the 60s, there was no way you could take over the USA without an army, and we knew that. It was never Malcolm X's or Martin Luther King's attitude to say, we're gonna take over the USA. We just wanted to make things palatable, so we could live in the country. That's what we were fighting for – decent living conditions, education, the elimination of racism.

"We still are. The whole race question has not been resolved yet by any means."

Max Roach has been fighting racism and drumming like thunder for nearly half a century.

Sixty this year, he's a tall, dignified man; soberly dressed, very courteous. The hair is speckled with grey, the eyes peer through thick lenses, but he looks fit and trim; the back still ramrod straight. He's been boss of the beat for 40 years, from bebop to hiphop, and for nearly as long has been an outspoken champion of black freedom and civil rights, dedicating much of his time to that cause.

The whisper is that Max Roach is a *serious* cat; but such a heavy reputation takes little account of his soft-spoken charm, his gentle humour. If he leans over at times to tap my sleeve like a pedagogic family elder, the gesture comes with a disarming smile.

He was born in New York in 1925, and first came to notice as part of the bebop scene that flourished along 52nd Street in the mid-40s. Playing with young bloods like Charlie Parker, Dizzy Gillespie, Thelonious Monk and Bud Powell, Roach became one of the main architects of bebop, the man who – together with the slightly older Kenny Clarke – turned the rhythm around to cope with this radically new kind of music.

Building on Clarke's innovations (chiefly switching the beat from hi-hat to cymbals), Roach laid down fast, flicking polyrhythms that suited bebop's convuluted lines and freed the rest of the kit for punctuating or 'colouring' purposes. This allowed drummers to be more versatile, and by the 60s free musicians like Ed Blackwell, Elvin Jones and Sunny Murray were no longer just timekeepers, but solo voices on equal footing with the horns.

Roach's first major recordings were with Charlie Parker, on the latter's Savoy and Dial sessions of 1946-48, but the first significant lps under his own name came six years later, when he formed a quintet with the brilliant young trumpeter Clifford Brown. The Brown/Roach group, which featured firstly Harold Land, then Sonny Rollins, on tenor, rapidly grew into one of the quintessential Hard Bop outfits, famed for their hard, immaculate blowing on lps such as *Jordu*, *Study In Brown* and the live *At Basin Street*.

Together with Art Blakey's newly-formed Jazz Messengers and the Miles Davis/John Coltrane quintet, Brown and Roach wrested jazz back from its drift towards the laid-back attenuations of the Cool School and reasserted its black cultural roots in blues and gospel music.

Then, with the group barely two years old, tragedy struck. On a rainy night in June 1956, Clifford Brown and group pianist Richie Powell were killed when their car slewed off the Pennsylvania Turnpike and crashed.

Roach struggled on, leading the group through various personnel changes, and also running the Debut record label with bassist Charles Mingus. When he finally found a suitable replacement for Brown in the equally young and gifted Booker Little, a second tragedy followed: Little, a phenomenal trumpeter, died of uraemia in 1961, aged 23.

By this time, Roach had become involved in the black political scene, and his records began to reflect his eloquent espousal of the Civil Rights movement.

Between August 1960 and September 1961, working with musicians who included Eric Dolphy, Booker Little, Coleman Hawkins and singer Abbey Lincoln (later his wife), Roach recorded three lps that laid down the blueprints for two decades of black protest music: *We*

Insist! Freedom Now Suite, Percussion Bitter Sweet and Lincoln's *Straight Ahead* tackled the issues of racism and sexism, saluted the guerilla opponents of South African apartheid and celebrated the heroes of black history – Roach's 'Garvey's Ghost' predating Burning Spear by 15 years.

Roach didn't just use lyrics to make his point, he allowed the music itself to be shaped by political meaning. He explained that the track 'Man From South Africa', with a turbulent 7/4 rhythmic undercurrent, helped to "express the anxiety, frustration and conflict involved in the struggle for independence." (In fact, his drumming underwent changes at this time, the dense, multi-ticking cymbal beats giving way to a lean, less-textured, more rhythmically variable style.)

His upfront radicalism brought a swift response from the establishment. Roach was vilified by many white jazz critics, who accused him of fanaticism and reverse-racism; and his name was placed on an unofficial record company blacklist. For five years, no label would record him. (This attempt to silence Roach was only partially successful: he took his groups into the studio at his own expense, and still hopes one day to release that material.)

A second result of the smear campaign was that even the musicians he hired were, at first, wary of him.

"I remember when Freddie Hubbard first joined the band," he tells me. "After he'd worked with me for six months or so, he came up one night and said, 'You know, Max, you're not a bad sort of cat after all, but when I told people I was gonna join your band, they said, man you can't go with Max, that guy hates people, he hates whites, he hates the record industry, he's heavy'."

Roach shrugs mildly. "I was surprised that people said that. It wasn't true. Just because I said that music can be used for something other than entertainment—"

He seems remarkably untouched by bitterness or regret.

"Well, I was on the front line with it," he says. "I was marching in the freedom marches, I was deeply affected by the whole thing. I still am. I'm concerned about what happens— my forefathers were slaves, my grandchildren may not live long because of all this crap about the Bomb. I can't forget those things."

So was your music intended to bring about political change? *Can* music do that?

Roach shakes his head. "No, I don't think that's possible. But I can use my music to offer another opinion, so to speak." He leans forward, lays a finger on my arm. "See, the illusion is that art is for the sake of art, that it has nothing to do with the rest of the world – art is over *here*, politics is over *there*. For me, that's not true. I believe politics is into everything.

"Art is a very powerful weapon, it can take us all out – we escape into *Dallas* or into disco, the illusion that life is a big party, and OK, maybe it's necessary to take a break. But if you take people right away from reality, from the problems facing us – like the Bomb, and unemployment, and the conservatism that exists today – that just serves the purpose of the ruling class, because it means the mass of people are not involved in any of the decisions that effect them and their lives."

So how would you answer those people who claim jazz and politics don't mix?

Roach laughs. "How could it *not* be political if you live in a society like the US and you're black? The music itself was born out of neglect— if you survived. I mean, Charlie Parker growing up in a racist society, that manifests itself in the music. You didn't have to talk about it, you were aware of what was going on in society – no jobs, no education— this is what jazz is all about. I think jazz itself *speaks* of that.

"If you listen to the blowing of a Johnny Hodges or the wailing of a Bessie Smith, if you go right back to the old Negro spirituals or right up to what Anthony Braxton and Cecil Taylor play today, you can *hear* in the music that these people speak of their socio-political situation. Whether it's overt or very subtle, it's always there."

The remarkable thing about Max Roach is that he's *played* with Johnny Hodges, he's *played* the old spirituals, he's *played* with Anthony Braxton and Cecil Taylor. Alone of the musicians of his generation, he's still seeking new challenges: while Art Blakey and Dizzy Gillespie continue to bebop and Miles Davis sticks with funk, Roach – as well as leading his own groups – has worked with gospel choirs and string quartets, co-founded the percussion ensemble M'Boom and recorded a stunning series of duo lps with avant-gardists like Braxton and Taylor.

So why all this diversity?

"If you're a creative artist, you have to have new ideas." He frowns, the mild face transformed by a deeply-furrowed brow.

"If I had to play like I played with Bird for the rest of my life, I couldn't stand myself. To me Anthony Braxton and Cecil Taylor are as creative as Bird and Bud Powell, but with them it's a different musical situation, so it challenges me to do something else. With them I'm not so confined as far as the drums are concerned, I'm freer to find new ways of dealing with the instrument."

Some of these "new ways" can also be heard on the exceptional solo drum tracks Roach has recorded over the years, from 1966's 'The Drum Also Waltzes' and 'For Big Sid' to the six solo tracks on his latest lp *Survivors*. He's truly the complete drummer, adept at all jazz styles, still a master of cymbal play, and a keen student of African and Caribbean percussion.

He's also very interested in working with voices, a facet of his history that ranges across Abbey Lincoln's dramatic scats on *Freedom Now*, the wordless chorales of *It's Time* and the spirituals sung by The Institutional Church of God in Christ Choir on 1971's *Lift Every Voice And Sing* lp.

Perhaps the best-known of his recent projects is 'The Dream', a track from the *Chattahoocheee Red* lp, on which Roach solos around extracts from Martin Luther King's famous "I have a dream" speech. It's a highly charged piece – and it predates 'No Sell Out' by years! Even so, I was surprised to hear that a few months back he'd played a local SoHo rap, scratch and breakdance show with Fab Five Freddie.

"Yeah," he grins, relishing the memory, "Fab Freddie's father and I grew up together in Brooklyn, so there was a great age gap and a great musical gap—I was very hesitant at first, but it was fabulous. They had three turntables, and the way they kept the pulse going, a snippet of this, a snippet of that, it was *out there*! It was very political too; they wanna say something about what's happening to their lives. I think it's real."

It is this belief in change, which has seen Max Roach through 40 turbulent years, that lies at the very heart of his philosophy.

"Black people in the US— see, each generation comes up and they cry out for change, and it reflects itself in the music." His finger taps insistently against the table top.

"I look at Louis Armstrong, he wasn't a schooled musician, but he became a great trumpet player. To me, he's like a rapper today: he didn't have any social benefits, but he came up with something – and, like a phoenix out of the ashes, here comes jazz, here comes rap!"

The image clicks. It sums up the Roach view of jazz: a tale of birth and rebirth, struggle and hope. Out of the ashes came Charlie Parker, Bessie Smith, Anthony Braxton. Out of the ashes came 'The Dream', Martin Luther King crying *"let freedom ring"* as Max Roach flails cymbals like the tolling of a great, celebratory bell.

On the streets, in the soul, a phoenix rises.

March 1985

BETTY CARTER
In Her Own Sweet Way

I tell Betty Carter, I read a quote of yours where— I think you said you can be very aggressive.

"I am aggressive," she replies. "Not *can be*, I *am*. I am aggressive."

Er— is that through having to deal with the music business?

"No, no." She leans intently across the table. "See, the only difference about my being aggressive is that I'm a female. If a man's aggressive, we don't even talk about it, but he does the same things that I do to get to his goal, right? He works at it, tries hard— but if I do it, it sticks out like a sore thumb – 'the female's aggressive'. And aggressive for a woman is negative, but being an aggressive man is wonderful." She pulls a face at the incongruity, and unlocks a throaty chuckle.

"Independent is another one. Use that word with a female, and it's a negative – what it means is she's striking out and accomplishing things, doing what she wants to do, like anybody does. But because we're the kind of society that says females are supposed to be constantly *demure*, and please don't ever say *no*— it's like, I've just had problems in Germany because the men there think they can do anything they want and you're not supposed to say NO to them. And because I said no, I became a dirty— well, a *difficult* person. Me!" She puts on a mock-demure expression, then breaks into a big grin.

"You know, saying no is *aggressive!*"

Betty Carter may not be difficult, but she has formidable presence. A small, stocky woman, smartly attired today in yellows and creams, her slightly rolling gait somehow lends a magisterial air, and her piercing glare could turn you to stone at 100 feet. She also has an extraordinarily mobile face, and a set of comically sour and sly grimaces acts as a kind of meta-text to what she says. She's witty, forthright, very much her own woman: it's quite in keeping that one of her best-known songs is 'I Can't Help It (That's The Way I Am)', a self-penned composition that includes the lines *"Have you considered what it does to your soul/You sell it when you play some other's role."*

I ask if feminism has shaped her views at all, but she shakes her head and says, no, life has.

"Just hard work. I had a family to raise, I didn't want to become a prostitute, you know, I didn't want to go on welfare. I didn't want to do anything but *sing*. That meant I had to fight for it; and I wanted not just to be an ordinary singer, I wanted to become an arranger, to do things differently, to make my music interesting. So I had to study, to learn; I had to not mind getting out there on stage and sitting in. That's what I had to do."

So she did it. Betty Carter might have had to fight for it for the last 40 years, but today the results are looking good: she's raised two sons (much of the time, single-handed), she's established her own Bet-Car record company, and her art has matured to the point where many aficionados consider her the greatest living jazz singer – a performer who combines the authority of Bessie Smith with the artistry of Billie Holiday, whose live shows range from the intensely dramatic to the wickedly funny, and whose brilliant scat solos contain some of the most inspired bop-based improvisation this side of Charlie Parker.

It was with Bird, in fact, that her singing career really began. Born Ella Mae Jones in Flint, Michigan, in 1930, her first serious foray into music was as a high-school bebopper who skipped classes to catch Parker's afternoon shows at Detroit's Palace Theatre and who "adjusted" the age on her birth certificate so she could see him at the city's nightclubs.

"You had to be 21 to get in," she smiles, "but we *had* to see him. So, yeah, I forged my birth certificate and missed school, really being a very *bad* girl, but I loved that music."

And when someone told Bird she could sing, he invited her up on the bandstand.

"So I sang with that band – Miles Davis, Max Roach, Duke Jordan, Tommy Potter – and after that, every time I showed up, Charlie

Parker would ask me to sing. That was the kind of encouragement I got from him."

If Carter's fierce love of bebop first drew her into the music, that loyalty also brought problems. After she left school, she played around bars and theatres in the mid-West then, in 1948, she landed a job with Lionel Hampton's big band – only Hamp was from the swing school and definitely *no* bopper. As Carter once told writer Michael Ullman, "He would do things like get on the bus and ask me— 'Hey Gates, whose band you like the best, mine or Dizzy's?' — And I'd say, 'Dizzy's'."[1] But Gillespie, then fronting the premier bebop big band, wasn't hiring women, so Carter stayed with Hampton, using the time to learn about music – reading, writing, arranging.

Her relationship with Hampton grew increasingly stormy: he actually fired her *seven* times during the two-and-a-half years she toured with him, but each time his wife Gladys, who liked Carter's voice, rehired her. Still, Hamp got his revenge; ignoring her preferred pseudonym of Lorraine Carter, he'd introduce her every night as "Betty Bebop" – and the Betty has stuck.

In 1951 she finally left the Hampton big band for a residency at Harlem's Apollo Bar, and she's been independent for most of the last 35 years, working nightclubs and – in the 50s and early 60s – the black theatre circuit.

"There was the Apollo in New York, the Howard in Washington, the Royal in Baltimore, the Regal in Chicago. You'd do three or four shows a day, and this way, if you didn't really know what you were doing, by the end of the tour you'd have a pretty good idea," she laughs. "That was *training*. It was what we needed, what every young artist needs, to find out where they want to go."

The tours in those days were truly *package* tours – half-a-dozen or more acts, each given a 15-to-20-minute spot, and assembled with little regard for the niceties of musical compatibility.

"I toured with Miles Davis, Ray Charles," Carter remembers, "with all the pop stars – The Orioles, The Flamingos, The Miracles, The Temptations, Gladys Knight And The Pips – with Muddy Waters, T-Bone Walker, John Lee Hooker. The works!"

You toured the South in the 50s? I ask. Before the Civil Rights movement started?

"Yeah, it wasn't until the 60s that the Civil Rights thing got heavy. I toured the South with Hampton and with Mantan Moreland in the early 50s; we did camp shows at that time." She reflects a moment. "The 50s were— well, you were still *afraid*, you had to stay on the wrong side of the tracks."

So you were playing to all-black audiences?

"Oh, sure. Mind you, when I was playing up North, I was playing to all-black audiences. It wasn't until the 60s that we really spread out. Black music was still called race music at this time, and white people did not buy it – or if they did, they had a black person to buy it for them, and then *hid* it. It wasn't until the mid-60s that the whites began to *admit* that they were inspired by black artists, because all the time before that Elvis Presley never mentioned the black artist. But The Beatles did, and that's what turned everything around, 'cause they were bigger than Presley. It was The Beatles who did it—" She sees me smiling. "You're proud of that, huh?"

You bet. I was a big Beatles fan. That's how I got into music.

"Well, The Beatles *said* they were inspired by black artists, and after that more white artists came along and admitted it, and they all started singing and talking like black artists."

She laughs her deep, throaty laugh. "They're still singing like us, and now some of 'em can do us better than we can!"

Betty Carter herself remains inimitable.

She paces the stage, hardly ever still, talks to the band – leading them through changes, geeing them through solos, charging herself on their energy; she paces, scats, paces, freezes momentarily in a set of grotesque poses – face screwed up, elbows out, fingers slowly clawing the air – as she suspends time, stretches tension to breaking point. She sings like no one else; a style characterized by startling intervallic leaps – the high, bright tones suddenly swooping to the lower ranges of gruff – and astonishing extremities of tempo, as rapid-fire scats alternate with ballads slowed to standstill, their silences explored for every scrap and nuance of feeling.

Highly personal, theatrical, brilliantly effective, it's also a style which, Carter insists, does not transfer easily to record.

"I've always had problems with being in a studio, in a cubicle, where all the musicians are far removed from me and there's not that closeness you get when you're all together. I like being close to people – an audience makes me *think*, makes me reach for things I'd never even try for in a studio."

Her response has been to ensure that most of her recent recordings are live; notably her *pièce de résistance*, the two-lp Bet-Car set *The Audience With Betty Carter*, which boasts (among others) an hilariously rephrased 'Trolley Song', a beautifully lugubrious 'Everything I Have Is Yours', several originals and one whole (25-minute) side of improvised scat. Still, studio albums such as *Now It's My Turn* or the second *Betty Carter* lp sound perfectly good to me; the only problem I find with Betty Carter lps is that they're nearly all unavailable – including one of her most famous recordings, the lp of duets she made with Ray Charles in 1961.

"That was a frightening experience," she recalls. "I was relatively unknown then, I just had a little puff of a name in the New York area, and here's a big rock star asking me to come out to California and record with strings and voices. I mean, I was very *scared*. Like, numb."

I raise a sceptical eyebrow. You don't *sound* scared.

"You don't believe me, huh? It's true, I was petrified. Literally numb."

Listening to that record today, it's the arrangements which sound petrified, but the singing – by both parties – is magnificent, particularly on 'Every Time We Say Goodbye' and the lp's hit single 'Baby, It's Cold Outside', a bravura performance which succeeds in being both funny *and* extremely soulful.

In the 50s and early 60s, Carter had recorded for several labels – Epic, Peacock, ABC, United Artists, Atco – but, feeling misunderstood by a music industry that tried to mould her into a commercial pop singer and unable to find a label willing to deal with her on her terms, she decided to start her own record company. In 1969 Bet-Car Records came into being, and she has since released four lps on the label: the first two both called B*etty Carter*, then *The Audience With Betty Carter* and, most recently, *Whatever Happened To Love*, a live album with trio and strings.

There were also, in the mid-70s, three short-lived lps on the Roulette label.

"Oh boy," she sighs, "that's a whole other story. I had to go to court on that one, that was one of my *bad* times. Somebody stole some tapes and sold 'em to Roulette – that's how they got *Finally* and *Round Midnight*. What Roulette did was offer me some money to do one album, and then tell me later that they had these tapes— you dig? So that's a subject I don't like to talk about. It's kinda *heavy*."

The record you did with them was *Now It's My Turn*?

"Yeah. But I didn't name it that. I *never* would have named it that." She pulls one of her sourest faces.

Presumably you prefer to stay with your own label now?

"Well, nobody's jumping over themselves to ask me to record for them; Columbia's not after me, Warner Brothers aren't after me. And they won't be unless they find a producer to produce me, and that's almost impossible 'cause everybody's *younger* than I am," she chuckles. "So how they gonna tell *me* what to do?"

Over the last 15 years the Betty Carter Trio has acquired a reputation as a training ground for young musicians: John Hicks, Curtis Lundy and Kenny Washington are three examples of Carter alumni who have made names for themselves. Her current trio – Benny Green (piano), Tarik Shah (bass), Winard Harper (drums) – are both very good and very young, just 22, 23 years old; so is it a deliberate policy of hers to hire young musicians and train them?

"Pretty much. The older musicians don't have the energy I like, and they're not adventurous. Younger musicians— well, they might make a mistake, but it might be a *good* one. You can learn a lot from mistakes."

And although Carter feels her own music has now gone beyond her bebop roots to a more personal – and contemporary – plane, she still maintains that Charlie Parker's music is the best foundation for a musical education: you have to learn the tunes and the changes, she says, and is bitterly scathing about the music of the 60s and 70s – fusion, modal and free.

"When we got into free music, musicianship went down the tubes. That's why Archie Shepp is now trying to play tunes," she laughs. "Really, it's as simple as that. See, he started out playing free, now he's trying to play a melody or two. But it's harder now, 'cause he put the cart before the horse. You should learn from the very beginning, when you're young, because when you get to 35, 40, who wants to practise?"

This seems a little hard on Mr Shepp, who, after all, was playing Ellington ballads in the mid-60s; however, I have other arguments I wish to pursue.

The men in your songs, I say, trying to sound nonchalant, they're nearly all unfaithful or very fickle.

"Oh no," she protests, " you haven't listened to my whole repertoire. You're just thinking of that one tune, 'Most Gentlemen Don't Like Love', right? I didn't write that, Cole Porter wrote that in the 30s; it's just a funny song, to make people laugh – don't take it seriously. I mean, if I sing "*Most gentlemen, they don't like love, they just like to kick it around*" – well, if the shoe fits—" she grins, "that's *your* problem."

Later that night—

It's dark in the club. A single, pencil-thin spotlight shines down on the floor where Betty Carter is stalking to and fro in front of her trio.

"*Most gentlemen, they can't take love,*" she sings, "*'cause most gentlemen can't be profound.*"

Some syllables she draws out, rolling them around her tongue; others she snaps short. The phrasing, the timing, are immaculate. The very air tingles.

She's into the mid-song rap.

"*So if your boyfriend, some fine night, should say, I'll love you forever and part from you never, now ladies it's your turn – kick HIM.*"

A female voice at the back whoops approval.

Carter laughs and looks along the line of front tables. Her eyes meet mine.

"See," she yells to me, "the aggressive woman is *in!*"

June 1985

---

1. Michael Ullman, *Jazz Lives* (New York: Perigee, 1982).

HORACE TAPSCOTT
A review of
The Tapscott Sessions, Vols 1-4
(Nimbus NS 1581/1692/1703/1814)
Recorded: June 1982-April 1983

Feminist writers have recently stressed the importance of 'naming' – a process as significant for what it *ex*cludes – and their insights can, I think, be usefully applied to jazz history. Take the term 'West Coast Jazz'; that it should be generally seen as pertaining to the work of a specific group of musicians, mostly white, mostly prominent in the mid-50s, effectively obscures a real, historical West Coast jazz tradition, which is mostly black and which has evolved, in post-war years, through such players as Wardell Gray, Teddy Edwards, Dexter Gordon, Hampton Hawes, Gerald Wilson, Harold Land, Sonny Criss, Eric Dolphy, Ornette Coleman, Bobby Bradford, John Carter, David Murray, Arthur Blythe, Horace Tapscott— I could go on.

Obviously, most of these players are *known* (though not all to the extent their work merits), but they are rarely viewed together as part of a socio-musical continuum called 'West Coast Jazz'. That name was already in use elsewhere.

It may have happened inadvertently, it may be that racism and media-manipulation got up to their usual dirty tricks, but the end result is that a transient white style has overshadowed a strand of black musical history by stealing its name. It's grossly misleading too, because to speak of West Coast Jazz without speaking of (say) Sonny Criss, Bobby Bradford or Horace Tapscott, is to speak a lie.

Tapscott, one of the most influential West Coast figures of the last 25 years, is little-known, at least in Britain. To be briefly biographical: he was born in Texas in 1934, moved to Los Angeles aged nine, first played piano, switched to trombone until a car crash affected his embouchure, then reverted to piano, made his professional debut with Lionel Hampton in the early 60s, but since 1961 has been mostly resident in Los Angeles, where he founded both the Underground Musicians Association (which later became the Union of God's Musicians and Artists Ascension) and the Pan-Afrikan Peoples Arkestra.

Tapscott's role in the Los Angeles music scene seems to be analogous to that of Muhal Richard Abrams in Chicago: he assembled a pool of musicians, took the culture to the community and laid down a solid basis for the nurturing of local music. It worked too: although based in Watts – long one of the most economically-deprived inner-city areas of America – the UGMAA and PAPA are still going strong, still playing free community gigs in parks and churches, 24 years later.

Tapscott himself has grown into a pianist, composer and arranger of prodigious talent. An early glimpse of this talent comes on Sonny Criss's fine 1968 lp *Sonny's Dream* (Prestige), which exclusively features Tapscott songs and arrangements. Criss, a superb and sadly under-rated altoist, often included Tapscott tunes on his lps; Arthur Blythe, a PAPA member in the 60s, has also acknowledged his debt to Tapscott, and they recorded together on the latter's 1969 quintet lp for Flying Dutchman, *The Giant Is Awakened*. But it was only with 1978's solo *Songs Of The Unsung* lp for Interplay, and a subsequent series of Arkestra recordings on Nimbus, that Tapscott's work began to be documented in any detail. Since then there have been four small-group lps (which I haven't heard), a duo lp with drummer Everett Brown Jr, and now this series of four solo piano recordings which, typically, features both Tapscott compositions and five works by "other unknown black composers in the Los Angeles area". This co-operative spirit is fundamental to his philosophy; the Arkestra lps, for example, all bear the declaration "Our music is contributive rather than competitive".

Tapscott has cited his mother (a stride pianist), Art Tatum and Andrew Hill among his chief playing influences; Duke Ellington and Gerald Wilson as models for writing. But the impression on *The Tapscott Sessions* is of a richly individual stylist, well aware of the entire piano tradition. He has all the things you'd expect – firm rhythmic grasp, clear sense of structure, blues and gospel feeling – yet it's also a music of surprises, of elaborate little asides, sudden sidesteps, playful dynamics, all stemming from a personal language that can be terse, dramatic or lyrical, as required.

Most of the pieces here are between four and nine minutes long; the longest is the 30-minute 'Struggle X – An Afro-American Dream', a bristling account of (I guess) black history and aspiration that traverses reflective spaces, pounding agitation and one chilling, inside-the-piano crescendo. It's not a music of extremes – no Cecil Taylor torrents or Ran Blake droplets – but Tapscott mines his middle ground for a goodly haul of stylistic shadings and emotional nuance: foreboding, 'The Tuus'; rhapsodic, 'This Is For Benny'; a Monkishly-dissonant 'Lately's Light-Green Blues'. 'Shades Of Soweto' embraces anger and tenderness, 'The Hero's Last Dance' is both manic and sad. Some tracks are complex, turbulent explorations ('Reflections Of Self', 'After The Storm'), some lighter, instantly attractive tunes ('A Dress For Renée', 'Toward The Sunset'). All carry the authoritative touch, the sense of *rightness*, which denotes a true master.

Tapscott has said that "most of my originals deal with people I have known or the experiences of Black people in America". *The Tapscott Sessions* are filled with such people, such experiences: Benny, Kopkee, Renée; blues, dances, struggle, dream. The music *names* them and in doing so celebrates their history, their community, their culture. This is another kind of naming; the reclamation of what has been denied. To the unsung, Horace Tapscott gives back their songs.

published September 1985

Steve Lacy

Chris McGregor *(above)*; Betty Carter *(right)*

Mike Westbrook *(above)*; Max Roach *(right)*

Sun Ra *(above)*; Marilyn Crispell *(right)*

Jimmy Giuffre

THE GUEST STARS

Ironing In The Soul

"The best accolade a woman singer used to get was that she sang with balls," laughs Guest Star Laka Daisical. "Rather a contradiction, I think."

Quite. Language is a weapon too. Reading a few old Blue Note sleeves recently, I noticed that Dexter Gordon's sound was described approvingly as "masculine", Ike Quebec's as "virile" – seemingly innocuous epithets that hide a knotty tangle of assumptions about gender, sound and value that leaves this writer rattled and confused. How, for example, do you describe a woman tenor player whose sound is similar to Gordon's or Quebec's? Where are the words for a specifically *female* kind of strength? Can strength, or sound, even be differentiated on a gender basis? Why is it (supposedly) a compliment to tell a woman she plays like a man, but an insult to tell a man he plays like a woman? The sexist bias of language extends down into biological metaphor: 'seminal' denotes great importance, 'hysterical' a freakish aberration. (One could even speculate on the relationship between male sexuality and male musical structure, like how come a piece of music is generally allowed to only have one climax?)

If these anomalies can reduce a relatively privileged male writer to teeth-gnashing perplexity, imagine the havoc they wreak on female writers and female musicians trying to find an authentic means of expression in what is basically – dare I say – *male*volent language.

"I'm forever trying to find the female style of playing the drums," grins fellow (aaargh!) Guest Star Josefina Cupido, drawing on her umpteenth cigarette of the evening. "Well, I say that as a joke, but I don't really know— I often think about that in relation to my instrument, because you do have to be so overtly physical to play the drums, and given the fact that all the music that has gone before has been written mostly by men – the way the rhythms have developed and so on – it *is* male music, I think.

"I sometimes feel I actually don't have the ability to play— hard funk, for example, which to me feels a very masculine sound, very aggressive." She shrugs. "I often feel inadequate on my instrument, and I know that has to do with technique, but then in a sense I don't know what technique is – like, who made all the rules and the standards— it's men, isn't it? So it's very difficult. I find it hard to play something that is absolutely rigid and consistent – is that because it's an essentially male sound? Because I'm a woman? I just don't know where those lines begin and end."

"I think a lot of drummers would find it oppressive to be called a timekeeper," frowns Daisical.

"But it's also implicit in the job," Cupido argues. "I do know it's taken a long time for me to play my instrument assertively, because women are not taught to be assertive. I don't know how it applies to other instruments, but with the drums it's clear because, in society, like, men hit things." She sips her coffee reflectively.

Daisical, meanwhile, is sifting through some press cuttings. "Journalists are usually very careful how they write about us, but sometimes— oh, here's one: 'Linda Da Mango and Josefina Cupido combine to produce a wonderful tapestry'— now," she laughs, "is this *knitting* or what?"

Josefina Cupido and Laka Daisical are, respectively, drummer/singer and pianist/singer with the Guest Stars, a group of six women musicians who have rapidly grown into one of Britain's most popular, and most-travelled, jazz bands. Their lively blend of jazz, pop, soul, Latin and African musics has taken them from the pokey backrooms of London pubs to several international festivals and tours of America, Germany, Spain and (currently) the Middle East; meanwhile, the success of their first, self-financed lp has prompted a second, *Out At Night*, due for December release: achievements that, at their outset, the band had never dreamed possible.

The Guest Stars began life in the early 1980s as a trio of women musicians – Julia Doyle (bass), Sue Ellery (piano), Ruthie Smith (saxes) – who wanted to explore jazz and thought a good way of doing so would be to play each gig with a different assortment of guests, hence the band's name. Gradually the basic personnel expanded, proved relatively stable (the current line-up of Cupido, Daisical, Smith, guitarist Deirdre Cartwright, percussionist Linda Da Mango and bassist Alison Rayner has remained unchanged for the past 18 months) and the Guest Stars became, both *de facto* and by choice, a women's band. The political consequences of that decision have proved both exciting and problematic, and are still being worked through.

"We do try and work as a collective," explains Daisical, "and I think one reason we do that is because it's been part of the experience of the whole Women's Movement – in which we've all been involved – to come together to share knowledge, and to break down feelings of oppression and resentment at work."

"We *believe* in that process, too," adds Cupido. "That way of working is fundamental to how we want to conduct our lives. It's aspiring to have control over our own destiny – which has become a boring phrase, I know, but I think it still applies, particularly in the music business, which is traditionally the place where things get appropriated and packaged. It's difficult to do because our society is geared to individualism, our whole conditioning is that of struggling for your own area, whether that's a living situation or a working situation."

"It may turn out that our collectivism is our undoing in the end," agrees Daisical, "that collectivism and individual expression are mutually incompatible. I just don't know. I think the collective idea is easier to pursue in a jazz context because the way you put the music together involves so much trust, improvisation means you're listening and giving. But at the same time there are certainly six very strong pulls in the band, and I don't think anyone has the illusion that we're going to be together in five years' time."

The band's struggle for control has slowly extended across several different areas; for instance, their decisions to a) stop playing jazz standards and concentrate on original material; b) start their own record label rather than seek record company support; c) produce their own records; c) organize their own tours; and e) handle, as far as possible, and with the help of their administrator Debbie Dickinson, their own publicity, promotion and advertising. The fact that they are an all-women band has proved both a help and a hindrance here, bringing them some useful publicity but also a train of patronizing males – like the musician who told Cupido her solos would "sound more effective if I wore a dress", and the journalists and promoters who insist on calling them an 'all-girl' band.

"If you added up our ages, you'd realize 'girls' wasn't at all appropriate," Daisical remarks acidly. "My favourite publicity blurb actually dates back to 1978, before the Guest Stars, when I was in Soulyard. We were on a bill with both women's and mixed bands, but we arrived at the gig to find the promoter had billed us as 'wall-to-wall women' – you know, like walk all over them.

"Still, it bothers me just as much that in Germany now, for instance, the Guest Stars are referred to as a salsa band. That's equally inappropriate."

Finding the right words to describe the Guest Stars can be a tricky business, not only because of the sexist bias of language but also because the group's music is so eclectic. If their commitment to "leaving space for improvisation" reveals a basic allegiance to jazz, it's also true that they use many elements of pop structure and are adept at numerous styles, from gospel to calypso. Such diversity may be a strength – and the band's live popularity suggests it is – but it also brings criticisms: that the Guest Stars have no coherent musical identity of their own, that they are simply cultural magpies – in their own words, "the whole Western musician with flapping ears" syndrome.

"We do talk about whether it's becoming a weakness," admits Daisical. "The danger obviously is that it all becomes a pastiche, but I think we'd resist that. It is hard, as privileged white Western women, to get the balance right; to acknowledge the musical debt we owe to black people, to acknowledge our privileges as white people, and at the same time, to insist that we do have something to say. But that's not unique to us, an awful lot of white people have to contend with that if they're trying to express themselves in a true way.

"And, again, I think our diversity is also a result of our collectivism; it's inherent in the nature of the band."

Still, I think my one big disappointment with the new lp, I say, is that even the diversity has become predictable; it just sounds like a better version of the first lp.

"But that's precisely why I'm *not* disappointed," protests Cupido, "because it does sound like a *better* version of the first lp."

There's nothing new, no surprises, I complain. To me, the Guest Stars are much more enjoyable live than on record; a good night out, but less satisfying in the cold light of home listening.

"If that's true, it's probably very healthy," Cupido laughs.

"In terms of our everyday experience, we're very much a live band," Daisical points out. "If you look at the time we spend in a studio – a month around May 1984, about a month in September 85, the odd session, and that's it. The rest of the time is *all* live work, and that's really one of the main reasons why the Guest Stars exist. We're in the Guest Stars because we enjoy playing with each other live."

The converse of that, presumably, being that women who choose to make music their vocation have to make more sacrifices than men do?

"In some ways, potentially, yeah," Daisical considers. "Babies, in particular. We were saying on the boat back from Germany last night that if we were boys, the chances are that some of us would have babies at home and it wouldn't affect the amount of touring we did. Whereas, if any of *us* had babies, although I think the band could accommodate that, it would certainly make life a lot more complicated."

"I did make that decision when I chose to be a musician," Cupido agrees.

"It might be different if we were studio musicians," adds Daisical, "but it's a choice that men don't have to make, certainly. Personally, I don't want babies, so for me it's not a problem, but for other people in the band it's more of a direct choice."

If there are costs, at least the Guest Stars are doing what they choose to do; they have control. There are pressures on all women in jazz, but for a feminist collective they must be enormous: the Guest Stars are trying simultaneously to blaze political trails, develop musically, stay together and remain in touch with their populist roots. On top of that, they're also in what Daisical calls "the cleft stick" of keeping faith with the fact that they are *women* musicians, while also wanting to be recognized as *musicians* rather than tokens. One comfort is that, while women musicians may be relatively scarce, the Guest Stars are not alone.

"The reason I love festivals," remarks Daisical, "is that so much different music is going on, and it's nice to be just one different thing in a whole heap of different things. 'Cause I think we are different, but we're not Martians."

Back at the typewriter, the journalist is pondering that word *knitting*. A whole new area for debate opens up: domestic activity as musical metaphor. *Weaving* rhythms, *threading* solos, *cooking* bands. A *polished* performance, a *half-baked* idea. What can we glean here of the complex web of relationships between gender, language and sound? Not a lot, perhaps.

Still, it comes as no surprise to hear that the Guest Stars, never exactly the humourless feminists of male mythology, were planning to give away a free tea-towel with every copy of their new lp.

"In the end we couldn't afford it, the recording cost too much," sighs Laka Daisical. "But it's a great shame. I think maybe we'd have done better to record on a four-track and give away kitchen equipment."

How can you pan a group like that?

October 1985

MARILYN CRISPELL
At The Square Root Of Energy

There are moments of epiphany that can change a life. Thirteen years ago, alone one evening in a house on Cape Cod, Marilyn Crispell placed *A Love Supreme* on the turntable: she is still living out the consequences of the next few hours.

"I don't know what happened that night. Something in the music – its feeling, its energy – caught me. I became incredibly moved and kept playing it over and over and over. I knew I had to learn to play it for myself. It felt almost mystical, as if the spirit of John Coltrane was there, and I asked for help—

"Hmm," she pauses, a little uncertainly. "Maybe you shouldn't put that in the article. It could sound kind of— flakey."

It could. But then Marilyn isn't the least flakey person on the planet: on one occasion, for example, while touring with the Anthony Braxton Quartet, she spent 20 minutes trying to figure out how to open her hotel-room door (and then had to call room service to release her) – a tale Braxton tells with relish, asking, eyes heavenwards, "What can you do with a pianist who can play 13/2 but can't open a door?"

The 13/2 is what matters: beneath the abstracted air lies a pianist of prodigious talent, power, acuity. She reshapes Coltrane's tunes with an empathy that hammers at the secrets of his art: rococo lushness for 'Dear Lord', a fleet 'Lazy Bird' with abrupt Tatumesque elaborations, the pounding rhythmic collisions of 'Coltrane Time', 'One Down, One Up' and – the most breathtaking – her 'After The Rain', which begins with deceptive calm, then turns into a maelstrom of spiritual intensity.

Her own music is no less of a revelation. Within the blizzards of sound she can raise, each note falls clear, a unique and beautiful crystallisation. Listening to her play, I can believe this woman conjures spirits, calls up tempests, shakes the floor of heaven.

And she's worried that *she* sounds flakey?

A diminutive figure, softly-spoken, modest to the point of self-effacement, Marilyn Crispell was born in Philadelphia in 1947. She began piano at the age of seven, then moved when ten to Baltimore, a city Billie Holiday described as "famous for its rats". An industrial port with a large red-light district, heavily segregated, it offered a bleak environment for a teenage girl. "I felt really beaten apart by the way things were," Crispell has remarked, adding that she had "escaped into music".

Later she attended the New England Conservatory in Boston to study piano and composition; but, disenchanted with academicism, gave up music after graduation and worked in medicine. It took six years, and the break-up of her marriage, before she felt drawn to music again and began to sing blues "for emotional release" in a folk-rock group. About this time she met a jazz pianist who introduced her to the work of Monk, Cecil Taylor, John Coltrane: the evening that she heard *A Love Supreme* she knew she'd found her calling.

For two years she studied jazz harmony in Boston, then, encouraged by Charlie Mariano, she moved to Karl Berger's Creative Music Studio in Woodstock, where she stayed for several years – first as a student, then as a teacher – until Reaganomics forced its closure in the early 80s. It was here that she met Anthony Braxton, Oliver Lake, Roscoe Mitchell, Leo Smith (with all of whom she has since worked), plus her hero Cecil Taylor, whom she regards as "one of the greatest geniuses of the 20th century".

Crispell is clear that, while John Coltrane is her spiritual inspiration, it is Cecil Taylor who is her aesthetic role-model.

"I feel as if I'm on a very similar wavelength to Cecil in terms of musical aesthetics, and although I came independently to that sensibility – back in Boston, before I'd ever heard of him, I improvised like I do today – it wasn't until I heard Cecil that I realised it was OK to play that music. Like, yes, I *can* do that. Before I made that connection, I guess I hadn't the confidence, or maybe the vision, to do it myself."

Asked to name the chief similarities between her music and Taylor's, many people would point to their phenomenal techniques; the sheer speed, intensity and physicality of their playing. Crispell herself, after a moment's thought, simply says "the tonality".

Sorry?

"We use a similar tonality. Some people would call it atonal, but I don't believe there's such a thing as atonality. Everything's related. If you analyse it, everything's related to a certain tonal centre."

Her admiration for Taylor has led a few critics to classify her as an acolyte; but if she was once of the Taylor school, the power and beauty of her own music (as it's evolved through lps such as *A Concert In Berlin, Rhythms Hung In Undrawn Sky, And Your Ivory Voice Sings* and *Quartet Improvisation, Paris 1986*) show she is now very definitely an *ex*-pupil. So we should talk too about the main areas of difference between her music and Taylor's.

"I think the differences are more to do with who we are as people, our musics as expressions of our selves," she muses. "Hmm— I've been trying to simplify, to develop simple ideas, simple rhythms. I feel there's also a lot of Monk in my music, kind of a speeded-up Monk, a lot of African rhythms too, and Braxton's been a big influence – I've gained a certain concept of space from him, using space and silence as much as sound, and using different textures. Playing with Anthony has been a valuable education for me."

Braxton – with whom she has played in various group contexts for nearly a decade – has returned the compliment, saying of Crispell that "Cecil Taylor apart, she's the strongest pianist I know of. She has the kind of facility that's really awesome." Taylor himself, 30 years an iconoclast, has commended her for "not making any concessions" and recently hailed her music as spearheading a "new lyricism", an epithet which she accepts with a degree of reservation.

"It's an aspect of my work, but I don't think of it as a primary aspect. I see the primary aspects as energy, counterpoint, pointillism— but maybe I am getting more lyrical in my old age," she laughs.

Counterpoint ("the layering of rhythms, different lines coinciding") and pointillism ("the juxtaposition of parts, things bouncing off each other") are vital components of her musical concept, the chief reason she prefers to play ensemble rather than solo. "I love to play *against* rhythms, to play strong rhythms of my own against a strong rhythm. Even when I'm playing solo, I hear rhythms happening, as if

I'm playing to a silent rhythmic partner."

This dialectic of extremes, with little space ceded for any middleground, is the kind of creative tension on which Crispell thrives. Her description of music as *"singing furiously in delicate tongues"*[1] reiterates (verbally) the shocking juxtapositions that are a major attraction of her own work: though perhaps the most startling contrast of all is entirely fortuitous, namely that her small, seemingly fragile, frame can unleash such a fearsome, two-fisted attack, you'd swear she slept on broken glass and chewed nails for breakfast.

Yet it is energy, the remaining "primary aspect", which is possibly the key element of Crispell's music, both melodically and spiritually.

"I think of energy as carrying itself forward," she explains, "being directed but not decided. I almost always work with small compositional elements, out of which things develop, carried along by the energy. *Spontaneous* composition. I definitely don't think of it as chaos, yet there's an element of— mmm— stars shooting through the universe. Or a white noise out of which themes develop like threads of DNA." She bursts into laughter, gently sending-up my fondness for extravagant metaphor. (No Christmas card for her this year.)

And the spiritual connotations of energy?

"When you're really hooked into the music, you can reach another level of energy that goes beyond the mechanics of it, a feeling of going higher, to a non-mundane state. I think it comes from getting in touch with your own energy, or with the primal energy of the universe."

I read her Blake's lines from *The Marriage Of Heaven And Hell*: "Energy is the only life, and is from the Body; and Reason is the bound or outward circumference of Energy. Energy is eternal delight."

"That's great, wonderful. I think energy is all there is, basically."

Energy is certainly a guiding thematic principle behind Crispell's most recent recording, *Gaia*, a trio lp with bassist Reggie Workman and drummer Doug James, which is her masterpiece to date. Whereas on earlier group records (*Spirit Music*, *Live In Berlin*) the exuberance tends to spiral into chaos, *Gaia* successfully transfers to a group context the balance of form and energy so notable in her solo work. With Workman and James (both superb here) pulling out all stops to keep pace with

Crispell's wheeling imagination, the intensity and interplay are finely-honed, wonderfully sustained: three free spirits in dynamic accord. Crispell herself is the complete virtuoso; the speed and clarity of her touch are astonishing, yet her technique is always at the service of her musical sensibility, the energy shaped by the requirements of the form.

Gaia is based, very loosely, on a poem about Gaia, the Greek goddess of the Earth, by Ed Sanders (of The Fugs), with whom Crispell worked on an anti-SDI rock-opera, *Star Peace*. I say very loosely because she emphasises that the music is not programmatic; and, in fact, three of *Gaia*'s five sections had already been written before she saw the poem. As with other of her pieces inspired by poetry ('Stoic', 'Element Air— Leap'), the music is not intended to be a literal interpretation so much as a response to the feeling of the poem. "In a vague sense, *Gaia* is related to what I saw as the Earth energy of the poem— primitive, symbolic, sexual energy, life energy. But it was conceived and organised purely on musical terms."

Gaia could almost be a meditation on the dance of form and energy. If the first section (a startling textural collage which is totally acoustic and played in real time) evokes energy as formlessness, the next three parts move through the creation, celebration and dissolution of form, while the final section reaffirms the indestructibility of the life-force in a fierce, joyous climax. It's an elemental birth/death/rebirth cycle, profoundly sexual *and* spiritual, as variously explored by, say, *The Rites Of Spring* and *The Tibetan Book Of The Dead* (two reference points with which Crispell is well acquainted). For me, though, *Gaia*'s lovely open-heartedness and life-bristling positivity are best captured by another line of Blake's: *"Everything that lives is holy."*

For all its brilliance, it remains to be seen whether *Gaia* will help Crispell achieve her most urgent goal: work. Since the demise of the Creative Music Studio, she has been scraping a living, extreme poverty the price for "not making any concessions" in her music. In 1985, when I first met her, she told me she was saving up to buy a chair.

"You don't have a *chair?*"

"The last house I lived in we couldn't afford a table either. We'd just sit on cushions on the floor, eating out of bowls."

In the last three years her financial situation has, if anything, deteriorated: although she is now a regular member of the Reggie Workman Ensemble and has taken part in various projects, from Anthony Davis' opera *X* to a Pauline Oliveros piece for four pianists (on one piano!), gigs remain few and far between. Only help from her parents and part-time menial jobs have kept body and soul together. Last autumn she reached crisis-point: a planned European tour fell through at the last minute and Crispell found herself facing a winter with little work and less money. In despair, she has since teetered on the brink of giving up completely, but a feeling that "music is in my blood" keeps her hanging on.

Trying to explain her beliefs about music's spiritual power, she reads me an extract from her private journal, about "the concept of not fighting against the system, which at this point is descending into another Dark Age, rather the need to work from 'underground pockets of light',[2] the effects of which will eventually be cumulative. The artist is a shaman rather than an entertainer – in a society where this is no longer possible it can be preferable to go underground; that is, to stop being a public performer."

I demur. Surely it's better to fight back? To try, at least?

Crispell sighs. "It's hard to fight back when you're trying to pay your rent, your telephone bill—and you're made to feel a bum and a dog because you're not out there working at some secretarial job for 40 hours a week."

Who makes you feel like that?

"The whole society. In America there's very little respect for artists. You're considered lazy, a bum. And the music business is aimed solely at making money, it has nothing to do with anything spiritual or any higher values. Even if you do fight back, there comes a time when, if you feel you've done everything you can do, you simply have to withdraw and conserve your energy, your power."

Are you near to that point?

"I feel like I go in and out of it."

But you've not decided to give up performing?

"I decide about once a month. Then somebody calls me up for a gig, so I just keep doing it."

The degree to which her neglect is rooted in sexual prejudice has long been a fractious point between Marilyn and myself; I'm certain it's played a part, she remains unconvinced. "The musicians I've wanted to play with, like Anthony and Reggie, have never looked down on me for being a woman; I've felt only respect from them. But I suspect that that prejudice does exist within the music business, so— I don't know. I don't know what people say behind my back."

Well, it needn't be personal. The institutionalised sexism of the music business has deterred many women artists, and, in these circumstances, Crispell's insistence on playing her own music, on her own terms, can only be seen as inspirational and incredibly brave. Given the odds against her, it's not surprising if she sometimes dreams of other options – like dyeing her hair orange and forming a rock band!

When she first mentioned this, I assumed it was a fantasy born of desperation, but she is genuinely fond of some rock and African pop musics. So is she serious about playing rock?

"I've thought about it, yes. I'd love to play with people like Talking Heads, Sunny Ade— to play with their rhythms, to improvise my own rhythms against theirs. I've tried writing a couple of songs, too, blues."

Why blues?

"Because I was very depressed." She sighs deeply: "I don't want a big house with two cars and a swimming pool, but I would like not to have to live in rented rooms for the rest of my life. I'm 41, I've no money, no work. My music isn't played on the radio, most people aren't even able to hear it. Sometimes I wonder, just what *have* I achieved?"

The grapevine reports that a well-known pianist recently complained to Cecil Taylor about the pressures of the music business. "I wish I could play my own music," she grumbled.

Taylor looked up, eyebrows arched, and replied, "Well, how many lives do you think you have to do it in?"

He told her to go listen to Marilyn Crispell.

January 1988

1. A line from her poem, 'And Your Ivory Voice Sings'.
2. A quote from the film, *My Dinner With André*.

DAVE HOLLAND
In Pursuit Of The Cubist Bass Line

1. COLOUR

In 1973 Dave Holland said, "timbre has been the most important development in modern music".

In 1988 I ask him, why?

"Hmm. At that time I was looking beyond the notes themselves at the attack and timbre you gave them. How a note was treated in terms of sustain, vibrato; the kind of texture you gave a note, the colour – these seemed very expressive qualities to me.

"I think more recently my attention has been on rhythmic development in the music, and right now I'm most interested in resolution – the way the rhythm resolves, the harmony resolves. You know how you go along listening to music— I call it selective listening. It's like when you look at paintings. Until somebody points out to you the dimension of colour, say, you don't really see what's happening with the yellow and the red and so on. Then suddenly your eyes are opened. It's the same with music.

"My attention is on resolution now, and when I go back and listen to Charlie Parker's records, or Coltrane's, I'm hearing a lot of new things because I'm listening to that particular element in a more exact way."

2. PERSPECTIVE

He sits on the hotel room bed, an amiable, articulate man, not looking his 41 years. If such things mattered, you could describe him as one of England's premier musicians (though he has lived in America since 1968); a bassist and cellist renowned worldwide for a technique that allows him incredible speed and facility, yet without losing the sensitive, singing touch he brings to slower pieces. He's versatile too, perfectly at home with the structural complexities of an Anthony Braxton composition, the barn-storming roar of a Sam Rivers solo, the total improvisation of a Company gig. The music he plays with the quintet he's led since 1983 tries to balance all the elements, and frequently succeeds. Perhaps, in the exquisite busy-ness of the parts, the focus sometimes gets blurred; as if there were a shade too much air and fire in the music, a shade too little earth and water. But it is a matter of shading. The Dave Holland Quintet is one of the 80s' most accomplished groups, a paradigm of how the African-American tradition can be complemented by the discreet addition of European sensibilities.

He's happy to talk, too. Doesn't need much prompting. Tell me more about resolution, I say.

"OK, if you have a key of C-major, say, there are a lot of different ways to resolve into that key, resolving meaning returning to it. One thing is that you can return to it at different points in time, you can resolve early or late, anticipate it—the same with melody, rhythm. You can fake a resolution, create the illusion of resolving and not resolve. What I'm doing now is looking at these alternatives, ways to create resolutions which are not expected. Or at least that I wouldn't expect."

Such as?

"Well, it could be very simple. Something that sounds like it should resolve down, you resolve up. Something which sounds like it should resolve on the first beat, you make it resolve on the second-and-a-half. You're dealing with three elements – harmony, melody and rhythm – and how they mix with each other. Because the rhythm can affect the way you resolve harmonically, and vice versa."

You're basically talking about alternative means to structure music?

"Kind of. It's more content-in-structure, ie not large structure but detail-structure. An example would be Cubism: Cubism created certain line resolutions that we were not used to seeing – reversals of dimension, two perspectives at once. The same thing happens in music. In 'Donna

Lee', for example, there's a change, where the melody's still outlining an F7 chord, but the chord has changed to the B-flat-7, which is the next chord in the harmony. So Bird's melody holds over the resolution for an extra two beats before he resolves into the B-flat chord. That's a simple example of delayed resolution. And once you start to look at that kind of possibility, it gives you a lot of alternatives; you don't feel straitjacketed by the movement of the form."

But it means you have to work *within* established forms, I suggest. You need the framework of the expected before you can make the unexpected happen.

"Not necessarily, because you can create a form as you play. You can set up the expectation yourself, lead the ear towards *this*, then do *that*. It's like creating a visual illusion, or the way Picasso turned perspective around. You can do that with rhythm: make it sound like you're playing on one side of the beat. Bird did this a lot, too; he'd turn the rhythm section around, then jump back on the original beat!

"But by changing one aspect you create a new setting, a new way of looking at things. That's the value of resolution for me. I'm looking for ways to expand, things to keep growing with. I've been looking at resolution for 18 months, two years, and I'm starting to hear it— it's coming out in my playing. The nice thing is that it goes into all areas of music. It doesn't only work on changes, I can do it on a blues too, or in an open context."

3. LINE

Dave Holland was born in Wolverhampton in 1946; nearly died in New York in 1981. Like many jazz musicians his story isn't linear but takes off on tangents, loops, curious side-trips. He began as a rock guitarist, then trained as a classical bassist. In the 60s he played pop with Johnny Ray, trad with Wally Fawkes, jammed with Jimi Hendrix; in the 70s he played beside Colin Walcott's sitar, Vassar Clements' bluegrass fiddle (he may also be the only jazz bassist to have played on a Grammy-nominated Country & Western lp). In the jazz field, he's played with Chris McGregor, Derek Bailey, Anthony Braxton, Stan Getz, Sam Rivers, Kenny Wheeler, Barre Philips. Oh, and Miles Davis.

I guess everyone's heard about the night in 1968 when Miles walked into Ronnie Scott's club, listened to Holland backing singer Elaine Delmar and said, "I want you in my band". Two weeks later, Holland arrived in New York and the next evening played his first gig with Miles. At that time Miles' popularity was at a low ebb – Holland recalls concerts where barely 30 people turned up – but within a few months he'd turned to the jazz-rock fusions which, with *In A Silent Way* and *Bitches Brew*, were to win him an entirely new audience. Ironically, it was a change that Holland came to find restrictive, and in 1970 he and pianist Chick Corea left Davis and went on to form Circle, with drummer Barry Altschul and reedsman Anthony Braxton. When Circle too broke up the following year, Holland worked a while with Stan Getz; then rejoined Altschul, Braxton and ex-London colleague Kenny Wheeler in the Braxton quartet, which became one of the classic small groups of 70s new music.

4. MOVEMENT

I ask Holland for his response to Leo Smith's comment that Braxton opened up "a field of new rhythmic elements".

"Well, Braxton has a special view of the relationships in a band, how they work together. And particularly how form relates to that, compositional form; movement in space and time. I couldn't say what Leo had in mind, but rhythm is certainly one of the aspects Anthony has looked at in different ways. The concept that the rhythm doesn't have to conform to a strict pulse, things don't have to relate metrically but can be bounced off a pulse, or can use varying speeds rather than a consistent beat. Those aspects of speed and motion."

On Holland's recent quintet lps, *Seeds Of Time* and *The Razor's Edge*, there are compositions by Doug Hammond that also suggest an original approach to rhythmic movement. Hammond is a percussionist whom Holland met through the quintet's saxophonist, Steve Coleman: but what's the special quality of his writing?

"First, he uses a lot of interesting rhythmic vehicles for his tunes, what he calls drum chants. It's a sort of African concept, of there being a rhythmic chant that goes on in the music – like on the track 'Perspicuity'

– which the players relate to. The drum chant represents certain rhythms or accents off which you can play. But also, when Doug writes a tune with harmony and chord changes beneath it, he'll write a kind of rhythmic pacing of the changes that's very unusual: it'll have chords change in different beats, say, and juxtapose them in different places. It makes a very interesting form to play on."

5. MEANING

While he was working with Stan Getz, Holland also began to play with reedsman Sam Rivers and the players that assembled for his first ensemble record as leader – *Conference Of The Birds* (1972) – made up, he says, his ideal group: Altschul, Braxton, Rivers. "There was a real predominance of the fusion music, which was an offshoot of what Miles had been doing," he explains, "and I wanted to make a statement for another kind of music." *Birds* remains one of his best records: acoustic, abstract, yet totally engrossing, its classic status self-evident.

That group played some concerts together, but the contrasting approaches of Braxton and Rivers proved incompatible. Holland didn't want to play with anyone else; so, because he couldn't have them both in his group, he split his time between the groups that they led. Then, in 1976, when the double-bookings became impossible, he devoted his time exclusively to the Rivers band: a decision related, as had been his departure from Miles, to the pull of free improvisation.

"Sam's thing was wide open, we never played a note of music that was written in the small group. Sam used to say, play all the music, play vamps, play free, play everything. I said, well, this is the finishing school for me."

The finishing school finished in 1981. Holland had already left Rivers, taken solo gigs, was mulling over his next move, when he was stricken with a viral infection that attacked his heart: one of his valves was seriously damaged. Even after the virus had been cleared up, he had to undergo open-heart surgery to repair the damage. For several months, it was touch and go.

The brush with death focused his thinking, he says: previously a procrastinator, when he recovered he knew exactly what he wanted to do – form his own band, "reassert the music".

6. FORM

The first lp he made after his illness was the cello solo, *Life Cycle*. He'd already made a solo bass lp, *Emerald Tears*, in 1977, but his interest in solo music had started as early as the Circle era.

"Braxton would say to me, why not do some solos? So we started doing duets and solos in the set. I played a little guitar too, a little cello."

His cello playing, I remark, is very different from his bass.

"Well, they're different instruments. The obvious difference is the tuning, and that leads to different styles of playing because there's a different relationship between the strings. In terms of improvising, I play a lot more on the bow with the cello and I think I play more— not exactly romantically— I think I have more of a Western classical influence in my cello playing, it's where my love of Bartók comes through. And a sort of English folk thing too – melodies which have a typically English sound to them. The character of the instrument suggests that to me. The cello lends itself to a different type of melodic approach."

The "English folk thing" seems as much an element of his composition as his cello: as evident on 1972's 'Four Winds' as on 1984's 'Homecoming' (on neither of which he plays cello).

"That's true, yeah. I guess it's my roots," he laughs. "I wrote 'Homecoming' in England actually. I guess it's something genetic or deep down in my psyche. There are things that influence you that are inexplicable other than to say they're inbred."

He cites Ornette Coleman and Kenny Wheeler as the chief influences on his composition: Coleman for the strong melodic lines of his music, Wheeler (who plays trumpet with the quintet) for his harmonic imagination. But the first quintet lp, *Jumpin' In*, is dedicated to Charles Mingus, I point out.

"Yeah, I owe a lot to Mingus in terms of the spirit of the music. And the combination of freedom and composition in his work, the concept of ensemble improvising. But I don't see my style of writing as strongly influenced by him."

Is nature an influence? I hazard. I'd noticed that several Holland tunes have titles like 'First Snow', 'Sunrise', 'Raindrops', 'Under Redwoods'.

"Nature's an inspiration to me," he nods. "You see a beautiful thing – a flower, a mountain – it gives you a sense of— creation, I guess. And art and nature— it's important to me that art should reflect nature. The natural forms, the spontaneity of nature, its organic quality. You know," he grins, "nature's organised chaos, its random forms!

"The combination of freedom and control is something that's echoed in the best art. So it doesn't look like something that was forced, but which just grew. The seed was planted, then it matured. I have the same approach to working on music. I see it as a matter of planting certain seeds in your playing, then letting them germinate and grow."

Seeds Of Time?

"That's it exactly."

7. SPACE

Sorry, I'm out of space.

February 1988

SUNNY MURRAY
Is It A Bus? Is It A Tiger?

Sunny Murray is one of the most influential percussionists of the last three decades: the man who pioneered free-form drumming in the early 60s, playing and recording in groups with Cecil Taylor (*Into The Hot, Nefertiti The Beautiful One Has Come*) and Albert Ayler (*Witches And Devils, Vibrations, Bells, Spirits Rejoice, Spiritual Unity*). He also made a number of records under his own name, notably *Sunny's Time Now* (Jihad, 1965), *Sunny Murray* (ESP, 1966) and *An Even Break* (BYG, 1969).

Born in Oklahoma of Choctaw Indian ancestry – "one of the five black Indian tribes of America," he tells me – he currently lives in Philadelphia, where he leads his group the Untouchable Factor, sometimes featuring Byard Lancaster and/or David Murray, and also leads and writes for a large orchestra comprised mostly of Philly jazzmen. Ever an experimentalist, Murray has developed his own drumkit, adding resonators and other electronic gadgetry to the standard trap-set – "it's taken me all my life, I only earn dinner money". He has performed works by John Cage plus Varèse's *Ionisation,* as well as remaining one of the most exciting and inventive of modern jazz drummers.

I interviewed him in the spring of 1988, when he was touring the UK as part of the David Murray Trio.

i

A lot of people have heard a strong Albert Ayler influence in David Murray's playing. You've worked with both men – do you think it's a fair comparison?
"Dave likes Albert, yeah. I think Albert was one of his basic influences when he was very young – someone for him to deal with. But Dave is a manifold guy. Also, the way Albert played was so personal that there will never really be anybody to play like him. I think Dave is one of the best of the guys who were influenced by Albert – and he's still a growing player. Come to that, I think I'm still a growing player, too."
How did you start out? Presumably you didn't begin as an avant-garde player?
"When I first started playing, I was playing Dixie. Then I became a kind of neo-bopper, and from that I went into the avant-garde."
How did that happen? I mean, listening to those first records you made with Cecil Taylor, it's as if your free drumming suddenly came out of nowhere.
"It's amazing that you've been listening to those records. Those are good records, but they're not around now – it's like they're from the dinosaur era! But they were fundamental. At the time, Cecil and I introduced avant-garde music as a kind of everyday—not everyday, but we were trying to make it an acceptable form of music. Because, say, two years before that, there was no avant-garde on the planet.

"Cecil and I kinda ran into each other. I was trying to do my thing on the drums with the beboppers, 'n' it was cool, but they weren't ready to evolve that fast. Cecil was. He'd already been playing his form of avant-garde, which had adhered more closely to Monk, Herbie Nichols. But he was ready to move on and I provided an impulse in that direction. So we ended up playing together, you know, two young guys. We played for about a year, just practising, studying – we went to workshops with Varèse, did a lot of creative things, just experimenting, without a job. We got beat up, cursed out, kicked around. Called dirty names. Cecil got both of his wrists broke; I almost got run over a couple of times."
Who broke Cecil's wrists?
"Some gangsters. We had both been threatened."
Why?

"Well, this is very deep— but it was real. At that point, it was real. Cecil healed. He had a couple of operations and he continued to play. And I continued to play. But we had to come to Europe, 'cause it got so hot. We cut out and came here. And in Sweden I ran into Albert, hanging out. He heard us in a club and said this was what he wanted to play. He wasn't getting any work in Sweden. Nobody liked the way he played. The cats liked him, of course, 'cause he was a beautiful person and he could play blues and all that stuff, but he wanted to play *his* stuff and there was nobody to play with him. So he hooked up with the band. He didn't actually work with the band, but he was like *with* the band. I shared my hotel room and food with him 'n' that."

ii

Have you always been interested in drums, in rhythm?
"As a kid, from the age of nine to, say, 13 or 14, I was a tap dancer, a very good dancer. *Seriously* good. That guy Gregory Hines, the actor, I could dance like him when I was a kid. On waxed floors. My life had already raised a deep rhythmical sense. My mother, my sister and I used to win dancing contests, ballroom dancing – I used to have a white dinner jacket (*laughs*). We lived in the ghetto, but this was always like a royal occasion. We had cabarets, with James Moody's Orchestra or Charlie Parker's Orchestra, and maybe 1500 people would come, all very well dressed, and there'd be food, barbecues.

"So the concept of being very correct with rhythm has always been with me. And when I got to bebop, I had right away wanted to understand Max Roach, Art Blakey, Sid Catlett – so I went through that very young. When I ran into Cecil, I had all this artillery. I tried to play my own way of bebop and I sounded a little like Elvin Jones, though I didn't know him then and he didn't know me.

"I remember Cecil came into the loft one time – we lived in a loft next to each other at that period – and he said, go down to the Half Note, there's a group down there and the drummer's playing your shit and they are *bad*. So I walked down to the Half Note and there was John Coltrane, Elvin, McCoy, playing their asses off. I stood outside the joint and I got really depressed. I thought, 'This drummer's terrific, he's just the greatest drummer in the world. What will happen to me? He's playing my shit! I won't make a dime off it. He's playing with John Coltrane.' So I went back home and Cecil said, well, let's just play. And we zipped it open and we went free.

"Then, after about a year of experimenting, we came back on the scene to play. But there was no support for Cecil. Except from John, Eric Dolphy – those cats *knew*, they supported us. They liked me when I was young, John and Eric, we became friends. Matter of fact, Eric brought Tony Williams over to my house, and that's how Tony got to know me. So these people were comrades of ours, even though they were in the big clubs blah blah blah. John paid Cecil's rent for six months and he helped me out with my children."

A little while later, it seemed there was a whole school of drummers who'd been influenced by you – Milford Graves, Rashied Ali, Andrew Cyrille.

"Yeah, drummers like Milford and Rashied, they followed me around New York and listened. They came to rehearsals. Matter of fact, a couple of 'em drove me crazy. I used to hate 'em, but I learned to love 'em (*laughs*). Every time I came out of a studio, they'd be sitting on the step, like 'how you doin', Sunny?' But *no one* ever asked for a lesson or a class! Yet every night they'd be listening in the club, like 'hey baby!', you know.

"Later I thought, well, at least I can work and feed my family, the people have got used to the music, Cecil's become popular, and there's a few more musicians out there who might hire me. But these drummers blocked me. I thought, damn! Every time I play there's ten more avant-garde drummers out there and they get hired instead of me. I was in a pickle there for quite a few years. It took me a *long* time to like avant-garde drummers – I'd go, 'play bebop, man, give me a break!' (*laughs*)."

Do you think your American-Indian ancestry may have had any influence on your sense of rhythm?

"Oh, yeah. Time more than rhythm. Because Indian rhythms are always very free, but people don't notice that 'cause all they hear is— (*slaps out staccato beat*). But underneath that, once you get a pulse going, there's a whole lot of shit you can do then.

"When I was young, I used to study a lot of rhythms. I'd learn 200 different rhythms – technical rhythms, upbeat, downbeat. There was one point when I was playing with Cecil when I used to go to the zoo and write out lion rhythms, tiger rhythms, gorilla rhythms. I was getting kind of— obscene (*laughs*). But it was really happening— like buses. I used to tape the sound of buses and try to imitate them – say, the engine running on the bass drum. That frightened people. Not frightened them exactly, but they'd look around in the middle of the tune, like 'Huh! Is there a bus in here?' (*laughs*). At least it gave me a different way to hit the bass drum."

iii

I wanted to ask you about your cymbal sound when you played with Albert Ayler. You created this lovely wall of shimmering cymbal sounds. How did that come about?
"OK. I had really defined a very good open rhythm – I was trying to get away from the bass drum, as it was. I was trying to get into the rapidity of beats to produce the sensation of tones— like, if you take a piano and hit the same two notes in succession, you'll get a third tone, and this is what I was trying to do with beats.

"Then, when I started playing with Albert, I started to go for the cymbal groove. I'd had a bebop cymbal thing at first, but I knew with Albert I needed a different cymbal groove. So I'd been playing this new cymbal groove for about a year when we came to Europe – Albert, Don Cherry, Gary Peacock – and I heard a record Tony Williams had made with Miles, and Tony was trying to get into a cymbal groove – and it was *my* cymbal groove! I said to Albert, I'm gonna play the cymbals so fuckin' loud till there ain't no sound left! So there was no more sound left in the cymbals for nobody to find for six years – and by that time Tony had gone in another direction (*laughs*).

"I still do it now when I feel like it. It turned into a music, 'cause I had to deal with it— to find an equation to keep doin' it where it wouldn't fuck up the band. It had to have a certain speed, a certain frequency to get that *p-i-i-i-i-i-i-ng*. It became something, you know. It was hard to do, so I had to find a way to do it. For a long time I wanted to play like that, but I couldn't make no bread. I loved to play it, but you couldn't do it in a small club, it was just too powerful a sound."

It seemed to fit perfectly with Albert's vibrato.
"Yeah. I still hum Albert's vibrato sometimes. I still hum 'Ghosts'. I try to keep my voice a pitch above the cymbals and then bring 'em up to it at the end. But I didn't do it all the time, 'cause I thought I would completely isolate myself. I was worried about that after I did those BYG records."
You can play very delicately too. Do you find it hard to keep quiet?
"With Dave Murray I play slow ballads with mallets, and it's difficult, yeah, because your downbeat's always there and if you just play, like, *boom, boom, boom*, it'd be nothing. So you have to learn how to keep the floating quality of the sound, and at the same time maintain the definition and dynamics of the sound within the flow— a bit like a propeller."

iv

I'd like to quote a couple of things you said in the 60s, and ask if you still agree with them. The first is that "America is trying to destroy the music". Do you think that's still the case?
"Yeah, it's still the case. They still don't accept the most original forms of the music. There's never gonna be that recognition of a black man's work as a viable, acceptable form of art – not in the avant-garde, though I think at its best it's a pure, a true, music. It's never gonna be a clear path."
This is because of racism?
"W.E.B. DuBois said it's the problem of the 20th century, colour. The war is not about economics, the war is between colours. People don't like to look at it, because it's about hate, racism, segregation. People just think they're too fucking different, you know. Americans did the same thing to their minorities as the Germans did to the Jews – they did the same to the slaves and to the Indians. So there's a whole lot of blood on America's hands, just within the country.

"But it happens even within races too. Like, when I came from the farm to the ghetto, I was heartbroken for about two years – they beat me up, called me Okie, all the darker boys jumped on me every day; my mother and sister got into fights. I mean, we were treated *bad*. I had to become a boxer, I had to learn to be tough, so they wouldn't take my dinner money.

"And it was like that in new music, too. Me and Cecil, after what we did, we were tough. We would fight you. I mean, Cecil would beat you up in a bar if you tried to tell us you didn't like the music. First, I'd start it. If you said, 'Your music sounds like shit', I'd throw a drink in your face, then Cecil'd – *pow!* – he'd hit you with something (*laughs*). The club owners really enjoyed that. Some nights we'd end up playing to, like, two gay guys and a drunk soldier. I remember one night Roy Haynes came down. He said, 'What's your name?' I said 'My name is Sunny, man, and this is the next shit!' I mean, I was OUT (*laughs*). It was like, if you don't like our music, keep it to yourself – don't say a word; don't even snarl, motherfucker! We'd go into a bar, Cecil'd collar the piano, I'd take the sticks from the drummer, you know, 'Get off the drums, man.' They thought we were crazy, but we had to be like that for a minute, 'cause we wanted to play."

You also said that as you were getting older, you were getting closer to beauty.

"Exactly. In avant-garde music, the best of your time is when you get older (*laughs*). I just hope I can make it to 70 years old."

What is beauty for you?

"You mean in life?"

Life, music—

"OK, in everything— it's love, it's togetherness, it's strength, it's respect, it's prettiness, it's lightning, it's water, it's earth, it's youth, it's old age, it's death, it's transcendence to a higher form of energy and existence. Somewhere. That's what life is about to me. I've had my dark days of despair, we all have 'em, but I can dwell on beauty now because, though I'm not rich and I don't work much, I found that that was the way to get through my problems. I don't necessarily sit up all night and read the Bible but I understand what the Bible means. I understand what the Koran means, what the Bhavagad Gita means. I'm a Buddhist and I'm also an eternal optimist, most Virgos are. And I want a revolution in the world. A *serious* revolution – all the good gets rid of all the bad. I think life should be about happiness, goodness, kindness – but where do you get that? Those are my beliefs, and maybe I'm not too realistic, but I hope that's how things will be."

You said, too, the intensity of the music could change things. You still think so?

"Maybe not intensity in its musical form. I feel the intensity of our existence will continue to change things. So we don't lose the intensity, it's rechanneled in a different way."

So are there new priorities in the music?

"People listen to me now from another generation. They can't absorb what we were able to thrash out to each other in the 60s. In the 60s you could play *out* for a crowd, and they'd love it, 'cause that was then. Now the environment is different, so if you want to reach people, you gotta put out an *intensity of reaching*. Your human thing has to come out.

"I think there'll be another dawn for drummers, too. It's still a very new instrument, the trap set. There's a new dawn to come."

May 1988

JIMMY GIUFFRE
Coming In From The Cool

Someone must have been telling lies about Jimmy G, for without him doing anything wrong his career was arrested one fine morning.

Club owners shunned him; record companies didn't want to know him; compositions gathered dust on his shelf. From being a successful, acclaimed musician, he found himself edged farther and farther from the scene until, finally, he had to take a teaching job to pay the rent. Without a trial, without charges being brought, Jimmy G was sentenced to silence.

The silence has lasted, give or take a brief interruption, for 25 years. He's 67 now, a slight, almost frail figure with thinning white hair (a tuft of which perches, Dizzy-style, beneath his lower lip); a solicitous, softly-spoken man whose careful, chewed-over words tail into inaudibility and reveal less than the subtle language of his eyes, one moment glinting with humour, the next measuring you with a steely glance.

Ask him what he thinks lay behind that Kafkaesque blackballing a quarter of a century ago and he'll say, with a mild shrug, "Well, I got into the free jazz." Long pause. "And I didn't use any drums." Long pause. "So— some people didn't think it was jazz."

Ah. Someone must have called the *Jazz* Police.

Censorship by definition – "You can't do that, it isn't *Jazz*!" – has been the bane of innovative musicians from James P. Johnson to Anthony Braxton; but few can have suffered from its effects quite so comprehensively as Jimmy Giuffre, for whom, as he puts it, "the doors closed" in 1963. In the nine years prior to 1963 he made 15 lps as leader, in the 25 years since he's made just four. (This is what happens when you tangle with the *Jazz* Police.)

Born 26 April 1921 in Dallas, Texas, Giuffre began playing clarinet at nine, tenor at 14 and by 21 had received his Bachelor of Music degree. He continued to study composition for ten years with Dr Wesley La Violette (to whom he still refers as "my teacher") and, after a brief period with a symphony orchestra, turned to jazz in the mid-1940s, playing with various big bands and achieving early fame as the composer of 'Four Brothers', the tune made popular by Woody Herman's Herd. Though capable of playing in the honking R & B style for which Texas tenors were renowned, Giuffre found himself more attracted to the 'cool' school of jazz then forming on the West Coast, which was derived from the quieter, more rhythmically relaxed style of Lester Young.

Based in Los Angeles in the early 50s, Giuffre became an influential figure in this burgeoning West Coast scene, notably as a member of Shorty Rogers' Giants; though it was on two lps with drummer Shelley Manne that his penchant for experiment first caught the ear: on 1953's *The West Coast Sound* the brief, atonal 'Fugue' displayed his interest in avant-garde composition, while 'Abstract No 1' from 1954's *The Three & The Two* was one of the earliest recorded examples of completely spontaneous improvisation. Soon given the chance to record his own albums, Giuffre began to question almost every facet of jazz orthodoxy: *Tangents In Jazz* (1955) has a rhythm section which doesn't play regular rhythm and often doesn't play at all ("I've come to feel increasingly inhibited and frustrated by the insistent pounding of the rhythm section," he declared at the time); and his debut lp for Atlantic, *The Jimmy Giuffre Clarinet* (1956), pursued his fascination with sound-texture through eight tracks of diverse, highly original instrumentations that included woodwind quintet, clarinet/celesta duo and solo clarinet with foot tapping. His clarinet tone was remarkable too, delving into the lower registers to achieve what one critic called "a thick, soft, nightish sound".

His second Atlantic lp, *The Jimmy Giuffre 3*, initiated the series of trio recordings for which he is probably still best-known. The first trio comprised Jim Hall (guitar), Ralph Pena (bass) and Giuffre himself on clarinet, tenor and baritone saxes. Though apparently the next logical step after the rhythm-experiments of *Tangents In Jazz*, Giuffre tells me that the decision to go drummerless was partly force of circumstance.

"It came out of Debussy, actually, that Jim Hall group," he recalls in his quiet manner. "Debussy's sonata for flute, viola and harp. So Jim was the harp, Ralph the viola and I was the flute. I'd been looking for someone who could play great drums and also wanted to play more of a chamber-type music – and it was hard. I couldn't find a drummer interested in playing softly, in listening and resting. So I heard this Debussy piece, I liked it and I thought, well, why not the three of us."

The absence of drums led to mutterings among the more hidebound elements of the jazz community, but these were drowned out by the popular acclaim for 'The Train And The River', the lp's closing track, which became a surprise hit. To a degree, the song's deft interlacing of catchy folk themes, the nimble dance of three melodic lines across wide-open spaces, typified the trio's music of the mid-to-late 50s, even though their instrumentation underwent a further radical change when valve-trombonist Bob Brookmeyer replaced Ralph Pena.

These were busy years for Giuffre: he guested with the MJQ, wrote arrangements for Lee Konitz and Sonny Stitt, recorded his own notated works with Gunther Schuller and Orchestra USA and even made an album (*Four Brothers*) on which he overdubbed four tenor parts, thus anticipating the saxophone quartet by nearly 20 years. However, the trio remained his central activity, pursued through excellent lps like *Trav'lin' Light* (with Hall and Brookmeyer), *7 Pieces* (with bassist Ray Brown replacing Brookmeyer) and *The Easy Way* (with Red Mitchell replacing Brown on bass). Then came a slight hiccup – two lps at the turn of the decade found him adding a drummer to the group and seemingly uncertain of his direction: *Ad Lib* was a blowing album, *In Person* a live lp – before he formed a new trio early in 1961 with Paul Bley (piano), Steve Swallow (bass), and suddenly began to play the most adventurous music of his career.

It was almost certainly his three lps with Bley and Swallow that made Jimmy Giuffre a marked man in the eyes of the *Jazz* Police.

"I started getting more daring in my recording," he asserts softly. "I started with *Fusion*, then *Thesis*, then I let everything go on *Free Fall* – there's no time, there's no key, no metre. We just— I found the right people to play with, that listen to each other and aren't greedy. Everybody got plenty of room to play."

To what extent were these freedoms influenced by the innovations of Ornette Coleman and Cecil Taylor?

"I wasn't copying Ornette or Cecil Taylor. I mean, I got something from them, but my music— my approach has never been about fitting to what other people are doing. I don't know whether it's good or bad or what, but I've always tried to put my stamp on it – playing and writing.

"*Free Fall*, that group sort of evolved from— Paul and Carla were always after me to write more abstract music—" He hesitates a moment, suspicious of the terminology. "Well, call it abstract."

The music *is* more abstract, but the freedoms explored on those last trio lps represent a logical evolution from Giuffre's previous recordings and exemplify – as does his entire *oeuvre* – the credo first quoted on the *Clarinet* lp sleeve: "It has been said that when jazz gets soft it loses its gusto and funkiness. It is my feeling that soft jazz can retain the basic flavour and intensity that it had at a louder volume, and at the same time perhaps reveal some new dimensions of feeling that loudness obscures."

Ironically, it may be Jimmy Giuffre's quietness (musical and personal) which has caused us to overlook the more revolutionary elements of his music. Comparisons with Taylor and Coleman perhaps seem absurd; yet Taylor and Giuffre were two of the first people in the 1950s to question the tyranny of the stated beat (and came up with diametrically opposite solutions), while Coleman and Giuffre turned to melody as an alternative to bebop's improvising over the chord changes pretty much contemporaneously. Bley, who had played with Coleman shortly before joining Giuffre's trio, may have been a catalyst; but Giuffre's stress on the melodic line is evident from even his earliest recordings and, he says, originated in the teachings of Dr La Violette.

"His basic phrase was that the harmony is the result of the line. That is, unlike the opposite approach where you fit the melody to the given chords, the line creates its own harmony. You just write with the intervals in mind, either resolved or unresolved, and you learn how to juxtapose those together, co-ordinating the lines so that they can all be heard."

This emphasis on the line led Giuffre to suggest, as early as the mid-50s, that the instrumental parts in his trio were interchangeable – ie, that all the lines were equal: a concept of ensemble democracy well ahead of its time, and which came to fruition on *Fusion* and *Thesis*, two of the most perfectly-integrated and beautifully-realised small-ensemble recordings in all creative music. (Though perhaps not in *Jazz*, because as Martin Williams' sleevenotes to *Thesis* concede, "On the surface, at least, this music may not always sound conventionally like jazz." However, let me quote his conclusion too: "But only jazzmen of the skill of these players could improvise with such technical and emotional freedom, and yet make such cohesive and effective music." Quite.) Giuffre, Bley and Swallow weave superbly intricate, intuitive patterns together, creating a richly reflective music that, for all its softness, remains intense, disciplined and rigorously honest. If the absence of conventional rhythm is what made these lps seem so odd at the time, it's probably that which makes them sound so fresh and contemporary today. No other group from the early 60s (with the possible exception of the Cecil Taylor Unit) managed to do away with all the props and still achieve such a serene balance of form and freedom.

Verve, his label in the late 50s, rewarded Giuffre in the customary manner of record companies – by not renewing his contract. So the trio's final lp, *Free Fall* (1963), appeared on CBS; not that CBS deserve any kudos either.

"Teo Macero got behind that and made it happen," Giuffre murmurs. "But it was out of the catalogue again in three months—" It was, he adds, his favourite album. Available for three months; unavailable for 25 years.

Free Fall takes a step beyond *Fusion* and *Thesis*, the most free and abstract of the lot. It also shakes up the format with a mixture of solo, duo and trio tracks. The latter two are the expected seamless blend of composed and improvised, but the solo tracks – all for Giuffre's clarinet – are free improvisations. Had he, I enquire, been trying to develop a new language for solo clarinet?

He nods. "Yeah. At that same time I wrote a quintet – for clarinet and string quartet. I played it at the Library of Congress in Washington. That piece had a cadenza I played which was all improvised." He shoots me a rueful glance. "I've got a couple of those pieces— they don't have much chance of ever getting done."

There seems to be enormous hostility towards compositions by people from the jazz field, I say. Presumably your pieces have fallen victim to the same prejudice?

"Well," he mutters, eyes gimlet-sharp, "I don't see anybody rushin' to do 'em."

After *Free Fall* came the freeze-out: Giuffre was not able to record again for nearly ten years. The man who'd been a leader of the West Coast 'cool' school found himself cold-shouldered by the music business; run out of town by the *Jazz* Police for not playing loud'n'sweaty enough.

A brief flurry of activity in the early 70s – two lps under his own name, two with Paul Bley on the latter's Improvising Artists label – was followed by almost a decade more of silence before the two 1980s Soul Note lps, *Dragonfly* and *Quasar*, which have signalled his partial return to musical activity. Despite a late conversion to electricity – impressed by Weather Report, Giuffre now uses electric bass and electronic keyboards in his current quartet – the Soul Note lps display many of his characteristic qualities: delicate group interplay, acute attention to nuances of texture and timbre, a sense of spaciousness; the *rub* of thoughtful, intimate music. Yet neither these lps nor his 70s albums are as far out as *Free Fall*. Had he taken a deliberate step back from the edge? Or did he feel he'd taken free music as far as he could with *Free Fall*?

"No, not exactly. But, you know, the doors closed, I didn't record for ten years. I kept trying different things. Far out is one thing, but I'm more interested in, hmm, *expanding*. I try to reach for a deeper meaning. The last two albums may not be as far out as *Free Fall*, but—," he tails off with a shrug. Then adds, "I have some recent tracks that indicate a new step, I think."

In what way?

"Well, they're not totally different, but they reach into a kind of pathos, a sad feeling, almost like European classical—like Mussorgsky, that kind of dramatic quality. I—," he tails off again, frowning. Then, after a long pause, "It's pretty hard to describe music. I just try to write a classic every time I write. Whatever a classic is— something that has an indelible frame for it, it's clear, it's strong, it's confident. It need not be dissonance. The free jazz thing, you can decide no or yes, just play free music, period; let the wind take it and your fingers flap. But straight-ahead, I mean things that are solid and done with total confidence, even though it's maybe not so unusual tonally or whatever, can reach another dimension, too."

Recent tracks like 'Cool', 'Moonlight' and 'Spirits' certainly sound clear, strong and confident to me: classics every one. It makes you wonder what Giuffre might have achieved had he been able to record and gig regularly. As it is, excepting the occasional film-score commission, teaching has been his major source of income for the last 20 years. This, not surprisingly, is a sore point.

Teaching is your chief occupation? I ask, less than tactfully.

"No, no. That's what's difficult—" For the first time in our conversation Giuffre sounds agitated. "People have a tendency to think that when a musician is caught teaching, he's retired. There's nothing—" He looks up at me abruptly: "Can you imagine why I teach?"

Er, in order to survive and pay the bills, I suppose.

"That's the number one reason. If I didn't have to, if I had the means to survive without it, I wouldn't teach. I learn when I do teach, it's not a *loss*; it's just that there's only so much time in the day and I'd like to practise more, get more music done. I'm at a period now where, ah, the music is coming out a little slower. I can't sit down and just turn it right out."

He purses his lips reflectively. The room falls silent.

The amount of music lost to him, to us, in his 20-plus years of reluctant teaching is incalculable. Even now he has had to go to Italy, to the Soul Note label, to find someone willing to release his work. "The American companies have turned deaf ears to us," he says. "I sent tapes to the important labels, they told me they were over-budget." One consolation, at least, is that the attempt to squeeze Giuffre out of the history books has surely failed. His experiments with rhythm and line played their part in the music's evolution, and his concern with the nature of sound and its relationship to silence/space prefigured many of the structural advances made in the late 60s by the AACM. Now, with his two recent Soul Note lps (a third is planned for later this year) rekindling interest in his previous work, a new generation of musicians is starting to acknowledge his influence: John Zorn, for instance, recently interviewed Giuffre on New York radio and has cited the trio with Hall and Brookmeyer as a factor in his choice of Bill Frisell and

George Lewis for the *News For Lulu* project.

Giuffre gives a slow, appreciative nod. "You're out on an island, you know," he muses. "I mean, unless you go to clubs or concerts every night, or buy records to figure out what so-and-so's doing, which I don't, you're out by yourself on an island, you're not really connected to anyone else, and it's interesting, and nice, to hear that someone is—doing something."

Later, as I'm packing away my tape recorder, I ask him if he feels any anger or bitterness at his treatment by the music business. He considers for a minute, then gives a wry smile.

"No," he says, a glint in his eye, "I guess I asked for it." My surprise must have shown, because he adds, "I mean, it's not as if I'm the ultimate musician. There's still a lot I want to learn. New things I want to try."

At which point a cough comes from inside the wardrobe and a voice clearly says, "Nothing *too* new I trust, Mr Giuffre."

The *Jazz* Police are still among us.

November 1988

KENNY WHEELER
The Trumpet Shall Sound

There's diffidence and there's diffidence. It has taken Kenny Wheeler 40 years to edge painfully from one to the other. Back in 1973 fellow-trumpeter Ian Carr noted Wheeler's reputation as "an extremely shy person, undermined by self-doubt" – and to such an extent that, while first working with John Dankworth's big band in the 50s, he had supposedly "been so terrified by the idea of a broadcast that he regularly used to send someone to deputise for him – though he needed the money".

Now, in late 1989, I sit in the kitchen of his small, cosy terraced house in Leytonstone and wonder, is that the wind I can hear or are his teeth chattering? How is the famous nervousness these days?

"It's got a lot better," he avers softly. "I think the last— say, five, six, years I've started to relax a little bit, to feel more secure on the instrument. But I still freeze up now and again. It used to be a horror to me almost every time I played."

And the self-doubt? (This, remember, is the man who once remarked "I don't have any solos of my own that I like completely, only those that are not as bad as others.") Is there any of your work that you like now?

"Oh, the compositions, I'm often happy with them. I never listen to my solos, not often – I still cringe a little bit. It's not that I dislike them— well, some I dislike, but generally it's just that I don't have any interest in listening to them. But compositions are a different thing. I guess people don't really think of me as a composer, but to me it's just as important as the trumpet playing."

This hint of self-assurance is put into perspective when Wheeler explains *why* he likes his compositions. How do you approach writing? I'd asked. What sparks the initial idea?

"Hmm— I don't know— I'm not one of those people who walks along the street and the tunes just come to them. I wish they did." He gives me a rueful grin. "It involves spending endless hours at my piano. It's almost like shedding junk from your head and then, maybe, if you're lucky, something will happen. But you can't force it – it just comes when it's ready, if at all.

"I guess it comes from getting into this almost— what's the word?— *trance*-like state. It's like you're tapping into something that's going by – you just happen at that second to tap into it and get a tune out of it— whatever it is. That's why I like my compositions," he confides with a chuckle; "I don't feel they're mine at all. It's as if they've been given to me, so I don't feel bad about liking them."

It's a nice irony that one of the world's finest brass players should be so chronically hopeless at blowing his own trumpet. Even his current Contemporary Music Network big band tour, in celebration of his 60th birthday, was not his own idea, but was suggested to him by Jazz North West/Ah Um impresario Nick Purnell, a longtime Wheeler admirer.

It's extraordinary, given his history, that this is Kenny Wheeler's first UK big band tour as leader. He was born on 14 January 1930 in Toronto, began playing cornet when 12, and moved to London in 1952. ("I sort of had wanderlust," he explains. "I wanted to go somewhere exotic like Cuba or South America, but I didn't quite have the nerve, so—") So he found himself in London, delivering the Xmas mail as a temporary postman, before securing work as fourth trumpet in the Roy Fox big band. For the next dozen or so years, he was a regular on the big band circuit, his open-minded approach to music catching the attention of such diverse leaders as Carl Barriteau, Alexis Korner, John Dankworth, even Tubby Hayes – though Wheeler hastens to add that he wasn't much of a bebopper.

"I wasn't really good enough, at least not at bebop. And somehow I always had the feeling that although bebop is my roots, and what I always listened to, I wanted to find some slightly kind of other way for myself."

In the mid-60s, a few such ways – some more than slightly kind of other – at last began to open up for Wheeler. For one, he spent several months studying composition with Richard Rodney Bennett; for two, someone played him a Booker Little record and "that was like a door opening for me. I breathed a sigh of relief when I heard him because I realised there was another way – you could still have your roots in bebop yet not play just bebop."

But the third, and perhaps most influential, "other way" he explored came through his involvement in London's burgeoning free music scene. He played in the Spontaneous Music Ensemble; began a long (and continuing) association with Evan Parker; recorded with Tony Oxley on the drummer's pioneering *The Baptised Traveller* and *Four Compositions For Sextet* lps; and, on Parker's recommendation, was asked to join Alex von Schlippenbach's Globe Unity Orchestra – an invitation that gave him an *entrée* into the European arena.

When I remark that presumably the attraction of free music was that it offered the other way he was seeking, Wheeler demurs, claiming that he played free music primarily because the free players were the only group who asked him to play with them.

"I don't really know what the attraction was," he adds. "I must admit that the first few times I heard it, I really didn't like it. I went to the Little Theatre a couple of times, just listening, and I didn't like it. But then John Stevens, I think, asked me to sit in, so I did, and it was—almost *therapeutic* to me, the playing. I couldn't say whether it was good or bad, I just knew I got something out of my system."

Though Wheeler was concurrently involved in numerous other projects – small groups with Tony Coe and Alan Skidmore, the Joe Harriott/John Meyer Indo-Jazz Fusions, various big bands led by Mike Gibbs, Chris McGregor, John Surman, Mike Westbrook – free music remained a major focus of his activity for several years, and its influence on him can be gauged in the differences between his first two lps, both big band records: *Windmill Tilter* (1968, Fontana) and *Song For Someone* (1973, Incus).

"I guess *Windmill Tilter* is a bit more— I don't know what the word is— a bit more *tight*, maybe," Wheeler frowns thoughtfully. "In later years I liked a looser atmosphere, a slightly freer thing." This change he attributes to the impact of such free players as John Stevens, Derek Bailey, Evan Parker. "I don't know what would have happened if I hadn't met them. I can't imagine," he muses. "I'm glad I did meet them, and I'm glad of the influence they had on me." He allows himself a wry smile. "What happened was I became one of those people who was too far in for some, and too far out for others."

A typically self-deprecatory joke, perhaps, but it does point to Wheeler's unique location on the spectrum of modern trumpeters. Though he rarely plays free music now ("somehow the people I liked to play free music with seemed to get fewer and fewer"), he's too inventive and adventurous a player to fit comfortably within the confines of the post-bop mainstream. And intriguingly, though he cites Booker Little and Mongezi Feza as influences in freeing up his trumpet style, he traces his initial discontent with his own bebop chops to listening to saxophonists. "I'm surprised there aren't more trumpeters who play like saxophonists," he remarks.

By which he means what, exactly?

"I suppose the players I like most are people like Sonny Rollins and, say, Joe Henderson, who have this thing of not always playing *da-da, da-da, da-da, da-da* – they're all over the place, which I love. But nobody seems to do it on trumpet, and when I do it people think either I'm crazy or I don't know what I'm doing. People seem to expect a trumpet to swing and play dead on the beat and there are not too many trumpeters who get away from that. But that's what I'm trying to do, to play that loose thing."

When I ask Kenny Wheeler if he'd been aware of creating a *new* music in the London free scene, he shakes his head.

"No, I never really thought about it. I suppose I did when I played with Anthony Braxton – I realised that was something new because of the controversy it caused in the press. But, for me, I was just trying to play his music as best I could."

Wheeler first met Braxton in the early 70s, and later became a regular member of his quartet when the saxophonist signed with Arista. It's an association he looks back on with fond nostalgia.

"It was the best period of my life, really," he murmurs. "I love that period from 74 to, say, 76. I was really sorry when that quartet finished. I'd sure like to play with Anthony again one day."

Why was it the best period of your life?

"It was the first time I'd ever been involved in a *group* and I'd always wanted to do that – be involved in a group that was working and growing and all that. And to play with musicians of that calibre! I think Anthony is a great player, Dave Holland too – well, I'd played with Dave before, of course, so I knew him. I also liked playing somebody else's music who really knew what they wanted: Anthony's music was very difficult, but— he had a *conception*, you know. Plus I started to record for ECM at this time, I was writing all these tunes. It was a great period."

Wheeler's series of small-group ECM albums – *Gnu High* (1975), *Deer Wan* (1977), *Around 6* (1979), *Double, Double You* (1983) – firmly established him as a world-class trumpeter and composer; four lps of gloriously impeccable playing and finely-crafted tunes, often bucolic and/or romantic in mood. His own preference is for *Deer Wan* ("to me, it's the most *complete*"), though he agrees that "most musicians seem to like *Gnu High* the best", a choice with which I'd concur, chiefly for its feeling of intimacy, its assured sense of space and its typically relaxed Wheelerian pastoralism. But *Around 6* also fascinates; the most experimental of the records in terms of both a line-up that includes Evan Parker, trombone and vibraharp, and song-structures that range from the dramatic changes of the 12-minute 'Follow Down' to the charming, three-minute 'Solo One' that remains Wheeler's only completely solo recording.

Listening to these lps again, I wonder if his diffidence doesn't emerge (as it were) in the way each record seems to be coloured by the character of his front-line partners – Keith Jarrett on the rhapsodic *Gnu High*, Jan Garbarek on the reflective *Deer Wan*, Evan Parker on the freer *Around 6*, Michael Brecker on the shiny-smart *Double, Double You*. Or is it simply that Wheeler the composer doesn't really have a *conception*? Certainly his interest in composition has rarely extended into structural experiments.

"I was heading that way a bit on *Song For Someone*, I suppose," he considers. "But I'm just such a sucker for soppy romantic melody that I came back to those kinds of tunes. I try not to get too sweet or sentimental, but I'm always trying to write a beautiful tune, jazz standard-type tunes."

So is the relationship between improvisation and composition in his work the usual bebop thing of playing over the changes?

"Yeah, I've been accused of using too many chord changes," he laughs. "I'm very much into harmony, melody— I let the rhythm take care of itself."

Does he think his writing has changed very much over the years?

"I guess it's become simpler," he suggests. "Recently I was listening to Radio 3 a lot, I was trying to step over this line— not exactly *into* classical music, because that doesn't feel right to me; but, anyway, I couldn't do it. The line seems to be coming farther back. My harmonic world has become smaller and smaller. I don't mean I'm using major chords all the time, major triads, but— I don't know— maybe the line'll come so far back I'll go completely free again."

There's little evidence of this trait either on Wheeler's most recent lp, the lovely *Flutter By, Butterfly* (1987, Soul Note), where his melodic gift and harmonic invention soar to new heights; or on his current big band tour, which features some of Wheeler's most thoroughly composed writing to date.

"I've become fed up with the notion that the band plays a couple of choruses, then everybody sits there while someone solos for ten choruses," he admits. "I'm more into the writing now, into balancing it— When you hear Ellington, the band seems to be playing all of the time. I'd like to go towards that, to have solos integrated into the compositions."

The big band (which ECM plans to record) comprises many of Wheeler's oldest associates – several even played with him on *Windmill Tilter* and *Song For Someone* – and the line-up also reflects his preferred practice of bringing together players from different areas of jazz. It is, in fact, largely his regular band – except regular here means annual.

"I had a big band once a year with the BBC," he explains. "We've done one broadcast a year for about 20 years, but I never could get any live gigs with the band. I think we did three live gigs in those 20 years."

Current tour aside, the lack of a regular working band (big or small) has meant only limited opportunities for Kenny Wheeler to hear his compositions played (and fewer chances still to experiment); but just as galling has been the scarcity of any kind of work in England in recent years. Though he has plenty of occasional work abroad and has also been a regular member of several groups – the trio Azimuth (with John Taylor and Norma Winstone), the Globe Unity Orchestra, the United Jazz + Rock Ensemble and (until last year) the Dave Holland Quintet – UK concerts have been few and far between; a fact which, he admits, he has viewed with some bitterness in the past.

"Yeah. It was, you know— not earning any money in your own country. When you've seen so many hotel rooms, you get a bit fed up. I guess I thought that by this time in life I'd be in a position to pick and choose a bit, maybe stay home and write more. But it's not like that, you gotta keep working all the time and— all that travelling gets you down after a while. Ten days or two weeks I can just about take, but over that it gets hard."

How long are you away from home each year?

"Oh, probably four, five months at least."

Reaching the age of 60 may be a cause for celebration, but it seems it brings its anxieties too, especially in the jazz life. Especially when you're a trumpeter.

"I hope my teeth hold out for another ten years," Wheeler remarks. "That's the main worry for any trumpet player. When your teeth go, you're most likely finished. A lot of players get false teeth, but it doesn't always work so good."

What will you do if your teeth *do* go? I ask (the journalist as ghoul).

"God knows, I don't," he sighs. "I'd love to sit at home and write, I've always wanted to do that, but who's gonna hire me? I can play the piano a bit – maybe if I practise hard for six months I could get my chops up and find a job in a bar somewhere." He laughs at the thought, keen to dispel the momentary gloom. "It might all sound a little miserable; I don't mean to sound like that. I'm really quite happy in my musical life. All the stuff I do is good now."

Some of us would say it always has been. Do you still practise regularly? I ask. Three hours a day, he says: you have to – two hours just to keep level, the third hour to try to improve.

"Oh, it's a terrible job on the trumpet, keeping your lip in," he pulls a face, half-jokingly. "I think it's the worst of all instruments. Even the trombone is easier, because it's a bigger area—," he mimics blowing, "—but the trumpet's tiny! You have to love it."

Long may he love it and blow it. Happy returns to Kenny Wheeler, a gnu high in jazz trumpet players.

December 1989

LEO SMITH
A review of
Procession Of The Great Ancestry
(Chief CD CD6)
Recorded 28 February 1983

It's seven years since Bill Shoemaker, in his notes to the *Rastafari* lp, quoted Anthony Davis' comment that Leo Smith is "one of the unsung heroes of American music". There have been precious few chances to sing his praises since then: only two recordings, both released in 1986, both hard to find and both documenting the various stages of a transition (1982-1985) in which, as he later told *Ear* magazine, "—the group began to introduce a music with a more obvious rhythmic implication. I began to adopt and mix some elements of reggae, some elements of funk and electric music—"

Though Smith had long been a student of all musics, the decisive factor in these changes was his conversion to Rastafari, which, he said, prompted his use of song – and, presumably, more popular forms – in a desire to communicate his spiritual message more clearly. On the *Jah Music* cassette, recorded in 1984, the "rhythmic implication" is perhaps a bit too obvious: a heavy beat and wailing electric guitars create a few moments of visceral drama, but overall the music feels claustrophobic and has an out-of-kilter awkwardness that recalls those late recordings on which Albert Ayler also tried to channel a spiritual message into popular forms. However, by 1985, when the first side of the *Human Rights* lp was recorded, Smith appeared to have found the right balance, mixing electric guitar and his winsome vocals with the elegant spaciousness of his earlier instrumental music. Then came four years of silence.

Procession Of The Great Ancestry, because it was recorded in 1983 (but not released until now), doesn't so much break that silence as make it speak all the louder, not least by reminding us that Leo Smith has been responsible for some of the most incandescently beautiful music of the last 25 years. The cd catches him at the turning-point of his transition; in fact, it's mostly a valediction to his pre-Rastafari music, a last wander through those lovely, shimmering soundscapes he also conjured on lps such as *Divine Love*, *Go In Numbers* and *Spirit Catcher*.

If anything, *Procession Of The Great Ancestry* rises to new, almost ethereal levels of gracefulness. This is a music of ritual and blues, of space and light: Smith's long trumpet tones hover like golden arcs over the quicksilver brilliance of Bobby Naughton's vibraharp and Kahil El'Zabar's delicate trickles of percussive colour. Like his fellow AACM restructuralists, Smith handles silence, texture, dynamic with marvellous finesse; and though the music is steeped in respect for tradition – the longer instrumental pieces are dedicated in turn to Miles Davis, Booker Little, Roy Eldridge, Dizzy Gillespie – it is chiefly shaped by Smith's innovatory concepts of "ahkreanvention" and "rhythm units", alternative methods of structuring improvisation which the trumpeter has been refining since the early 1970s.

Intimations of future change enter with 'Blues: Jah Jah Is The Perfect Love' and 'Who Killed David Walker?', two brief, vocal/electric tracks whose attractive vigour anticipates the brightest colours of *Human Rights*. Still, it's the instrumental tracks which, for me, constitute the real splendour of *Procession Of The Great Ancestry* and make it one of Leo Smith's finest recordings. The spirituality they evince may be less specific than that of his Rasta songs (or of the poems in the accompanying booklet, written by Smith under his Rasta name of Wadada in 1988), but it is no less palpable: you can hear it in the title-track's serene ceremonial, in the poised lyricism of 'The Flower That Seeds The Earth', in the dignified exaltation of 'Nuru Lights: The Prince Of Peace' (for Martin Luther King). All confirm, moment by moment, Bill Shoemaker's contention that Smith "has chosen a course where aesthetic, political and spiritual diligence are the ordering principles".

Given the rather different principles that operate in the American record industry, that choice is a measure of Leo Smith's heroism – and perhaps explains the scandalous lack of new recordings of his music. Whatever the reason, such a silence hurts us all.

published April 1990

SUN RA

The Mysteries Of Mr Ra

"I've been sent here to help people. My mission is to try and save this planet. Mission impossible." Sun Ra

Talk about moving in mysterious ways.

The wisdom of the universe has been stuffed into a white plastic shopping-bag, and is now lying slumped against a backstage wall at the University of London Students' Union. I watch intently as an ancient black man with an ornate head-dress and a bright orange beard pulls a wad of papers from the bag and begins leafing through them.

"I got some copies made but the pages all mixed up," he mutters. "I gotta be careful I don't give you no pages I ain't got copies of."

He thrusts a sheaf of papers towards me and I take them with trembling fingers. Am I dreaming? What I am now clutching could be the journalistic coup of the century, the most sensational news story of all time: except for one small snag. What I have in my hands are pages from a book transmitted to Earth by beings from outer space.

You see the snag. I'm not even sure I believe it myself.

My companion has no doubts. "You can't get off this planet but two ways," he tells me. "You have to die off it or somebody rescue you. I can be rescued by spaceships. If I request rescuing, I can get it. If humanity won't help me, some other type of beings will land and take me away. I keep that exit open." He shoots me a momentary grin, but I'm starting to feel way out of my depth. Right now, I wish a spaceship would come and rescue me.

"I don't think this planet has treated me right," Sun Ra continues balefully. "They think I'm a joke, but I know what I know. They think

they just dealin' with an old man – but I'm not a man, I'm a spirit being."
That I can believe.

"I'm not really from this planet. I did something wrong on my planet and they sent me here to pay my dues." Johnny Griffin

It's five years since Sun Ra and his Cosmo Love Arkestra last touched ground in the UK. They're here now, in early June, for a brief, three-gig visit – Liverpool/Friday, London/Sunday and Monday – courtesy of left-field rock label Blast First, who last year released the subtly mind-scrambling *Out There A Minute*, a compilation of rare, late-60s Arkestra recordings.

Offered the chance to travel with the band, talk to Sun Ra, attend the concerts, I rocket into seventh heaven. Not only are Arkestra sets among the most spectacular and joyous of all music events – the band in their shiny, outer-space costumes dancing, chanting and blowing the entire spectrum of creative music, from Jelly Roll Morton to (new Ra favourite) Walt Disney – but I'm fascinated by the "Astro Black Mythology" Ra has created as a context for both his music and his life. To say that my one previous meeting with him – in 1983 – had changed my life would be a shade melodramatic, but he certainly set off several new trains of thought for me (some of which I'm still running to catch). Besides which, and all enigma aside, this man is *special*, his achievements nothing less than astounding and his story possibly the most extraordinary saga in all of jazz. As one time Arkestra drummer Roger Blank has observed, "Musically, Sun Ra is one of the unacknowledged legislators of the world."

So who is he? The mystery begins here. In various interviews Ra has claimed that he comes from the planet Saturn, that he arrived on Earth on a date that can't be revealed because of its astrological significance, and that his name is a secret – though he has admitted to using the names Sonny Blount and Sonny Lee and has stated that his parents' name was Armani, which, he says, "comes from ancient Egypt". Certainly the name Sun Ra derives from Ra, sun god of ancient Egypt, one of the poles of the Ra cosmology: although, with typically sly humour, Ra has also announced, "Sun Ra is not a person, it's a business name". Whatever the truth about his name, two independent researchers, Franco Fayenz (in his sleevenotes to an Italian issue of the Savoy lp *The Futuristic Sounds Of Sun Ra*) and Gary Carner (in his forthcoming book *Jazz Performers: An Annotated Bibliography Of Biographical Material*), both cite 22 May 1914 as Ra's birthdate; and it's widely accepted that Birmingham, Alabama, was at least his terrestrial point of arrival.

The facts he has revealed of his early years confirm 1914 as a plausible year of birth: he's spoken of his folks taking him to shows by the great classic blues stars – Bessie Smith, Clara Smith, Ethel Waters – and of listening avidly as a child to records by Fletcher Henderson's Orchestra and other early swing bands. Ra formed his own band in high school, toured the Mid-West in the early 30s, but then seems to have dropped into obscurity until the late 40s, when he turned up as house pianist/arranger in Chicago's Club DeLisa, where he performed for a time with his first idol, Fletcher Henderson, and also played with many other artists who were passing through.

By the early 1950s he was leading his own combos and establishing a reputation on Chicago's South Side as a bit of an oddball. A keen student of Egyptology, Hebrew, philosophy and science, Ra issued his own pamphlets reinterpreting facets of the Bible and prophesying the coming of the Space Age – electronic horns, men walking on the moon, etc. (It seems these insights were greeted with scepticism: tenorist John Gilmore, who's been playing with Ra since 1953, remembers people calling him "on the moon man".) By 1956 Ra had assembled his first Arkestra, and that year they made their recording debut for the tiny Transition label. When the label folded before a second session could be released, Ra set up his own record company, Saturn – one of the first artist-owned jazz labels and certainly the longest-running. For the last 35 years he has released the bulk of his music – probably 100+ lps – on this label, still a shoestring organisation run from the band's communal HQ and still issuing records in the plain white sleeves with (sometimes) hand-drawn pictures and titles that are now valued collectors' items.

Just as amazingly the Arkestra too have survived for 35 years, despite relocations to New York (1961) and Philadelphia (1968) and innumerable, if evocative, name changes, such as the Myth Science Arkestra, the Blue Universe Arkestra, the Cosmo Jet Set Arkestra and the Astro Infinity Arkestra. The list of illustrious Arkestra alumni reads like an A-Z of modern jazz: Marion Brown, Vincent Chancey, Charles Davis, Richard Davis, Robin Eubanks, Von Freeman, Craig Harris, Billy Higgins, Clifford Jarvis, Frank Lowe, Julian Priester, Pharoah Sanders, James Spaulding—there are dozens more. What's even more remarkable is that many members have either stayed for decades, most notably the brilliant saxophone duo of John Gilmore and Marshall Allen, both with Ra since the 1950s; or, at the least, have kept returning to the fold – take, for instance, current bassist John Ore, who first played with Ra in 1964, or trumpeter Ahmed Abdullah, leader of three bands of his own, regularly in and out of the Arkestra since 1975. Being around Ra, says John Gilmore, is like "being around a fast-moving vibration. You know if you go anywhere else, it's a slowdown – you'll start moving backwards."

But Sun Ra has not only maintained a big band and a record label through years of hardship and ridicule; he has also – and uniquely – maintained a history and a cosmology too. I doubt that any band in the world can match the range of music the Arkestra regularly spans in a single evening: blues, swing, classics by Henderson and Ellington, Monkian bebop, 60s freeform, Ra's own space-age electronics solos – the Arkestra's repertoire is no less than the complete history of black creative music, performed with a passion and a gusto that explode it out of the past in a blaze of living colour.

Ra's been a trail-blazer, too: a 50s pioneer of synthesizers and electronic instruments, of modal music and freeform improvisation; of looking to Africa for inspiration (and finding chants, raps, polyrhythmic percussion); of reasserting pride in black music and black culture (particularly through his championing of the big band tradition). His influence has seeped into every corner of modern music, from Funkadelic to Stockhausen to the Art Ensemble Of Chicago. More significantly, Ra's explorations of the links between music and mysticism sparked a new awareness of sound's spiritual dimensions; the healing power of music, its role as an agent of transformation and the roots of this knowledge in African mystical traditions are all aspects of a Ra mythology which many musicians, from John Coltrane to Albert Ayler to Anthony Braxton, have been drawn to investigate for themselves. And that Ra considers its spiritual force (rather than, say, improvisation) to be the defining essence of creative music is underlined by his comment to me that, "You might say that jazz came down from the sun priests in ancient Egypt, from the ones who were worshipping Ra. They had music, they could heal people— They most certainly experimented with music and sound."

"Into being in this universe some 43,000 years ago. Moved around and then was ordered to this Planet Earth by the higher forces— for the purpose of serving my duty as a Music Messenger." Malachi Favors

Sun Ra's "Astro Black Mythology", created around the twin poles of ancient Egypt and outer space, provides the philosophical foundation of his music, yet is rarely taken seriously: dismissed by his detractors as a bad joke, even Ra fans tend to see it simply as a good one. So what dark purpose does lurk behind the glitzy costumes and the gnomic utterances? I went in search of enlightenment.

•

Why are you so interested in ancient Egypt?
"Well, I deal with the foundations of things. Civilization started in Egypt. It had the culture. It had the truth, too. Another kind of truth, which the world will have to recognize – although it went another way after that Moses did his job. But it's proven that the world's in the condition it is today because of Moses, not Pharaoh."
Could you explain the phrase "Astro Black Mythology"?
"Astro black is about— Oh, something that's greater than the truth. So it's over in myth, it's hidden. Myth was here before history. When they started history the truth couldn't move, 'cause they put a lot of lies in there too."
But what do you mean by "Astro"?
"I'm talking about space. I'm talking about not being a part of this planet. They got this planet on the edge of chaos and destruction. Everything they got here is improper: it doesn't fit with the universal law, it's selfish and egotistical. People been misled, they deep in ignorance."
On your track 'They Dwell On Other Planes', who are 'They'?

"I'm talking about the universe, about worlds this world don't know nothing about. But they exist. And there are other beings in other dimensions, strange dimensions, and people here know nothing about it. But when they send those rockets up there and get out in the universe, they'll find out I'm telling the truth."

Could you explain why the planet Saturn is important to you?

"You have to feel what you are. As a man thinketh, so is he. I'm not of this planet, and I know I'm not. I'm comin' from somewhere else, another dimension."

Is that why you called your record label Saturn?

"I had to deal with Saturn, 'cause I feel that a lot of black people come from the planet Saturn. I got some literature that says so, but it's not out there on the bookshelves. So I felt I had to do something in the name of Saturn, which I did – I made the record company. And Saturn is a beautiful planet – it's most beautiful. The early black man and the Babylonians, they worshipped on Saturn's day – Saturday is named after Saturn. Why would they worship on Saturn's day unless Saturn is very important? So I put my equation together. Now, in Babylon, each planet had a different colour: they had gold for the sun, silver for the moon, black for Saturn. So black people are associated with Saturn – the colours black, blue and purple. There were black kings and Babylon was a black nation, and they built a temple to Saturn, but, of course, religions came and obliterated it."

•

Ra's cryptic references to Moses and religion offer further clues to his interest in ancient Egypt and suggest too that it is rooted in a cultural context rather than personal idiosyncrasy. In 1954 the African-American scholar George G.M. James published his book *Stolen Legacy*, in which he argued that much of the philosophy and science attributed to the Greeks had actually originated in ancient Egypt, that Egyptian mystery teachings had been suppressed by the early Christians and – perhaps most significantly – that ancient Egypt had been a *black* civilization (a fact ignored or denied for centuries by white academics: come to that, when did you last see a black Cleopatra on stage or screen?). Though by all accounts Ra was well into his Egyptian researches before James' book appeared, there are definite similarities between the two, not least a shared emphasis on Egypt as a source of black pride and the need for black people to throw off the influence of Christianity in order to discover their own history and cultural identity. (Remember, in Old Testament mythology, basis for most early spirituals and gospel music, the Egyptians were the *bad* guys.[1]) And it's at least a curious coincidence that it was also in 1954 that (according to John Gilmore) Ra's embryonic Arkestra first began to diverge from standard big band uniforms – by donning Egyptian fezes.

The importance of ancient Egypt's *blackness* is attested to by current Arkestra members. Altoist Marshall Allen answers my queries with, "Well, there are a lot of ancient Egyptians in America". You mean black people? "That's right. People from all over Africa are there. You gotta have some kind of identity." And trombonist Tyrone Hill (ex-MFSB) states it even more plainly: "Knowing about ancient Egypt makes me feel better as a person, 'cause those were black people. Our race don't know very much about ourselves. In America, education and the mass media tell you black people got nothing to offer, but we've done many beautiful things. Sun Ra made me aware of this."

That relatively few African-Americans have been so aware is something that Ra has attributed to the influence of a Christian religion that was forced onto the slave population. He's already gone on record as saying that Christianity made black people passive to racism and its ugliness; and when I ask him about this, his answer suggests a disillusionment with the black race which, I guess, has been slowly growing over the years, and which may explain why the ancient Egypt mythology tends now to take second place in his music to the outer space references. It's as if, as Ra's dreams of a transformation of black consciousness have receded, he has turned increasingly to outer space and its inhabitants as the only remaining hope for this planet's salvation.

"I looked at the condition of black people in America and I judged the tree by the fruit. They don't deal with culture, with progress – they back there in the past, a past that somebody manufactured for 'em. It's not their past, it's not their history. They don't see no fault with America, they want to be part of it. I ain't part of America, I ain't part of black people. They went another way. Black people are carefully supervised so they'll stay in a low position. But I'm not down there, yet I come from one of the most discriminating states in the whole world – Alabama. They don't know why I am what I am. And black folks know nothing about me, so they can't ask them.

"I left my family, I left my friends, I left *for real*. I left everything to be me, 'cause I knew I was not like them. Not like black or white, not like Americans. I'm not like nobody else. I'm alone on this planet."

"I must play music that is beyond this world." Albert Ayler

Whatever you think of its outer space aspects, Sun Ra's music, at its best, is irrefutably out of this world. Recent releases such as the swing-based *Blue Delight* (A & M) and the expansive *Live At Pit-In* (DIW) suggest the Arkestra are hitting a new peak to rival the extraordinary outburst of creative excellence in the late 70s/early 80s that gave us a cluster of great lps: *Blithe Spirit Dance, Disco 3000, Media Dreams, Omniverse* and *Sleeping Beauty* on Saturn, *Lanquidity* on Philly Jazz, *The Other Side Of Space* on Sweet Earth, *Strange Celestial Road* on Rounder, the live *Sunrise In Different Dimensions* on hat Hut and two superb double-albums on the Italian Horo label – *New Steps* and *Other Voices, Other Blues* – that feature an exceedingly rare Ra small-group, with John Gilmore, trumpeter Michael Ray and percussionist Luqman Ali. (Ra prefers working with big bands, the bigger the better: "I know exactly how to colour music in such a way I need maybe two or three thousand pieces to interest me.")

The three concerts I see confirm this hunch: the word is 'sensational'. The gig at Liverpool's Bluecoat Arts Centre – house packed, ecstatic audience whooping every solo – is a typical Arkestra sound panorama: frontstage instrumental duels; the band dippy-dancing through their space chants; Ra crooning 'I'll Wait For You' and 'I Dream Too Much'; flurries of smoking alto from Marshall Allen, strumming his keys like a guitarist; Ra, face abeam, twirling a tinsel wand and parading with a cushion on his head while June Tyson sings 'Sunset On The Nile'; plus there's the *funkiest* Ra chant to date – *"You gotta face the music, you gotta listen to the cosmo-song"*.

But the gig at London's Mean Fiddler is, perhaps, even more impressive, if only because the band reach the same heights in far more trying circumstances: the acoustics are dodgy, the stage hopelessly cramped (no room for processions or dippy-dancing here, alas) and Ra's electric piano conks out on the first song. Disaster looms, but soon the adrenalin is flowing, the band hit their stride with a wonderfully bloodcurdling 'The Forest Of No Return' and the second set turns into a non-stop scorcher. It's peak after peak after peak – Marshall Allen and Noel Scott exchange electrifying alto tangles, a raggedy version of 'Slumming On Park Avenue' (from the Fletcher Henderson repertoire) adds hilarious satire, Ra sings a heartbreaking 'Down Here On The Ground' (*"So if you hear a sound, way down here on the ground, my friends it's only me, trying to fly"*), then throws in stomping blues piano, and John Gilmore, after two relatively sedate evenings, rises up to blow a series of absolute gems, including one solo on 'Lights On A Satellite' that is utterly bewitching – a lovely, flowing, feinting line that takes him in and out of the tune with compelling invention. Then, as the band file offstage and the audience clap along, Ra raps out his farewell warning: *"You're on spaceship Earth, you're outward bound, out among the stars, destination unknown. Destination un-known. Des-tin-a-tion unknoooooown!"*

•

Is your purpose here to play music? Do you enjoy that?
"Well, I *have* to play for people. It's not about me enjoying it, I'm compelled to do it. If I had my way, I wouldn't let 'em hear me. I'd go out in the East and I'd be a camel-driver or something, and I'd be quite content, 'cause I found out that simple people are very beautiful. They don't have any prejudice or discrimination, they ain't tryin' to harm nobody, and I'm happier when I'm around people like that."
Could you explain why percussion has played such an important part in your music?
"That's 'cause I be hiding behind the rhythm, so folks can't hear me. I stay out of the way, 'cause they don't treat people right who are sincere. They don't have me at *all* – not even on record. I choose very carefully what I put out on records. They have not heard the real me and they never will unless they learn how to treat me properly as a spirit being. If they just be honest with me, then I be honest with them. Otherwise I'll be a

mystery, and this planet'll never make it.

"See, I created a vacuum on this planet. Deliberately. I could be the president of a college, I could be in Congress, I got the kind of mind to do it. But I stood back and, therefore, where I should be, I'm not! Now, there ain't no way they can replace this vacuum I created in human society. No way. 'Cause they don't know how many places I'm supposed to be in. I wasn't in those places. I bin studyin' 'n' things. I gave my so-called life to study and find out what's happening here, 'cause I really cared enough about humanity to do that. So you might say I gave up my life by never living it. I did the equation on it. I'm not where I'm supposed to be, in black society or in white society, and I planned it like that.

"Now they have a vacuum. Nature abhors a vacuum, so other things are rushing in there that're not too good. Fools rush in where angels fear to tread! So what they gotta do? They have to listen to what I have to say. I can tell 'em what to substitute for the vacuum I created. I'm a scientist. I conquered a planet without a gun. Simply by not being in place. You know, for want of a nail, a shoe was lost; for want of a shoe, a horse was lost; for want of a horse, the battle was lost. Well now, that can apply to me and my strategy to defeat a planet that's doin' wrong.

"They were trying to stop me, so I stopped myself. See, everyone needs to be successful, but I didn't need it. That's the first time it happened – a planned strategy to not be successful. I was sent here to help the planet But, you know, it's in more trouble than I ever dreamed, and maybe if I'd known how much trouble it was gonna be in, I wouldn't have stayed out of the way.

"So I have not contributed to humanity, except I did put some beauty out there. My music was beautiful and it told the truth, but concealed, so only I could unravel it. I didn't do that to hurt humanity, I was only trying to protect myself."

"It's an inner revelation that has come several times to me, that I have been educated on Sirius, that I come from Sirius." Karlheinz Stockhausen

That night, after the ULU gig, I hurry away clutching my handful of random pages from the space book. The book, some 500 pages long, and given to Sun Ra by "space people" during his 1989 trip to Turkey, is called *The Information Book* and is, says Ra, "more fantastic than any science fiction. It'll change you. You'll know it's the truth." I'm tempted to peek on the bus home, but it hardly seems appropriate: this is the kind of thing you read alone in a locked room at the dead of night, with a nervous glance over your shoulder in case there's an alien being scratching at the window.

At first sight *The Information Book* is baffling; a collection of messages beamed down telepathically from the space people to certain mediumistic "friends" on Earth. It has, primarily, a functional slant – advice, instructions, answers to queries, explanations about vibrations, frequencies, dimensions, etc – but comes dressed in what often sounds distressingly like New Age-speak – there's much talk of brotherhood, sincerity, "luminous and flowery paths". On closer reading, though, the book grows curiouser and curiouser. There's a diagram of the constitution of the universe, which is run by something called "The Centre Of Unified Reality Administration Mechanism", though with the help of other "Mechanisms" and various councils, such as "The Council Of Stars" and "The Council Of Pre-eminent Ones". There are also various "Missions", Earth coming under the jurisdiction of "The Sirius Mission", and there's a diagram of the Sirius double-star system as our local "focal point of the unified reality". The space people claim to have bases throughout the solar system, including underwater HQ here beneath the North and South Poles, and they have some kind of astro-technology that measures each person's essence, to see how sincere and positive we all are.

There's a lot about the different religions too, some complex numerology and occasional interruptions by beings from yet other dimensions, one of whom – "from a medium where the spiral vibrations end" – offers advice on how to combat cancer (avoid stress, eat raw green vegetables, do gymnastics, take plenty of minerals and be spiritually strong). And terrestrial musos will be interested to hear that, whereas on Earth seven notes comprise a scale, in outer space music seven scales comprise a note, which means that "we possess sound vibrations with much richer volumes, but on your planet your ear frequencies can not receive these sound waves. If these waves could reach you, your brains would become liquid."

But I bet what you're all dying to know is, will the planet be saved? Is there a future? Hang on to your space helmets! "The predestination of your planet has been designed till the year 2000. There are many difficulties and obstacles in front of you which you will have to overcome." But don't despair: "After the year 1990, your planet, which will be washed by cosmic rains which have been unknown to your planet till today, will make progress and improvements unknown to it and a selection foreseen by the plane which is in touch with us from the Divine Dimension, will be made. The nineth *[sic]* solar system will help you on this path."

So there you are: be sincere and don't forget your cosmic umbrella! Incredible truth or insane fantasy? You'll have to make up your own minds because, due to a cosmic lack of space, this article will now continue in a different dimension. But consider, if space people didn't write *The Information Book*, then who did? And why?

This is Starchild Lock signing off with a final quote from *The Information Book*, a tip on personal salvation and the flowers of infinity. Are you listening, Planet Earth?

"The door of Carena is the door which opens to ASCENSION TO HEAVEN— There are three conditions to pass through this door: INFINITE PATIENCE – INFINITE LOVE – INFINITE TOLERANCE. It is not easy at all to possess these three flowers. This door is opened only to those who hold these three flowers in their hands without letting them fade and wither, because your hands which hold these flowers are suns made of fire."

June 1990

1. At the same time many slave spirituals carry intriguing pre-echoes of the Ra cosmology: *"This world is not my home / This world is not my home / This world's a howling wilderness / This world is not my home."* This is a topic I am currently researching. – GL, 12/93

JOHN GILMORE
Big John's Special

I

"Sun Ra doesn't allow us to say that we were *born*. He says we *arrived on the planet*. I arrived on the planet in Summit, Mississippi, but my family moved to Chicago when I was three years old."

Now approaching his 60th birthday, John Gilmore is considered by many cognoscenti to be the finest tenor player currently on the planet, though in terms of popular recognition he still hasn't really *arrived*. A crucial influence on John Coltrane, who once begged him for a lesson, Gilmore's talents have often gone unremarked because he has avoided the spotlight, preferring to dedicate his life to playing in the Arkestra, the singular band put together – and held together for more than 35 years – by the even more singular Sun Ra.

Gilmore first met Sun Ra in 1953 and, with the exception of one eight-month break in 1964-5 when he replaced Wayne Shorter in the Jazz Messengers, he has remained with Ra ever since. Though he has occasionally recorded with other leaders – Paul Bley, Andrew Hill, Elmo Hope, Freddie Hubbard, Clifford Jordan, Pete LaRoca, Dizzy Reece, McCoy Tyner – most of his recordings have been with Sun Ra, and nearly all of these have been in a big band context. Which perhaps explains why John Gilmore's tenor genius is still one of the best-kept secrets in jazz.

A tall, lanky figure, who speaks in a pleasant drawl punctuated by chuckles and many a cheerful "yeah!", he proved an affable interviewee, happy to while away part of a train journey by telling me about his formative years and his first encounters with the mysterious Mr Ra.

Gilmore grew up in Chicago and began playing clarinet at the age of 14, later adding tenor during his time in the US Air Force. Brought up by his mother ("We were poor, lots of kids, a one-parent family") and unable to afford a college course, he had joined up in the hope of pursuing musical studies in the Air Force, but for some time racial discrimination kept him out of the service bands. "It was very much segregated. The fellow asked, were there any musicians in the crowd who'd like to try music? I jumped up, but he just bypassed me – he didn't even give me any consideration. So I went into the regular Air Force; no band."

Finally, after six months of unhappiness had culminated in him dropping an aeroplane engine on his foot, Gilmore protested and was posted to an otherwise all-white band at the Kelly Air Force base in San Antonio, Texas, where he played classical music when on duty, then slipped off after hours to play jazz in the local nightclubs. A highlight from this period is the night he sat in with the Count Basie Orchestra.

"We all went to see Basie; boy, he was swinging! The guys said, Gilmore, go get your horn! I said, *no*. But they went back to the base, got my horn and put me up on stage with Basie. I never will forget, 'cause they were playing blues in D-flat and I'd never played blues in D-flat before! I got up on the stage and my knees were knocking – whoooh – my stomach had butterflies. But they were playing so much all I had to do was blow a few notes and everybody put me on their shoulders, carried me off as the big hero and whatnot," he laughs. "That was a good experience – I remember Lockjaw Davis, Dicky Wells and all the cats were there. And here I am, an amateur, playing in front of them. Yeah, it was too much!"

Six months after his discharge, in 1952, he returned to Chicago and took a job with the Post Office. But the work proved so exhausting that Gilmore found he had less and less energy for music.

In desperation, afraid he might lose his talent altogether, he gave up his day job and decided to try to make it as a full-time musician. His friend, drummer Robert Barry, was playing in a trio led by an oddball pianist at a club called Shepp's Playhouse: when the trio's saxophonist, Pat Patrick, took off on a trip to Florida, leaving behind a dep who clearly couldn't cut it, Barry invited Gilmore to their next show. That night, fate was in a pleasant mood—

II

i. Ahmad in the phone booth

"Robert said, come on down to the gig tonight and bring your horn – the cat might like you, he might give you a job. I went down, played a set and the next night I went to work – Sun Ra hired me. After a while Pat Patrick came back, so we had four pieces. Then we added Richard Evans, a bass player, Julian Priester, trombone, Jim Hearndon, tympani. We were one of the first groups to use tympani. And we were one of the first groups to use the electric bass, electric piano, electric organ. Sun Ra was way ahead in electronics, even then.

"We built up to about eight pieces and we worked this place called Birdland. We worked there for over a year, sometimes five or six nights a week, and the club was doing wonderfully, but the waiters and waitresses stole all the money (*chuckles*). So the man didn't make any profits and eventually he had to let us go, and we only worked Monday nights. We stayed there for another year, every Monday night.

"Ahmad Jamal was working upstairs on Mondays. He used to come down and steal Sun Ra's stuff (*laughs*). He'd be sitting in the phone booth, listening to Sun Ra. That's where he got his ideas for 'Poinciana' and 'But Not For Me', 'cause those were two of Sun Ra's featured numbers, and Ahmad made his hits off those numbers. He'd be in the phone booth, listening all the time! He also used a drummer Sun Ra had more or less tutored – Vernel Fournier. And, of course, Richard Davis was with him; he'd played with Sun Ra, too."

ii. The name of the Ra

What was Sun Ra called when you first met him?
"We called him Sunny."
When did he first use the name Sun Ra?
"Well, he was working at the Club Delisa, I believe, in the late 40s, before I met him. And a fellow called Sammy Dyer was the choreographer and show producer there: he took care of hiring all the girls and the band. Sun Ra used to rehearse the chorus girls before they'd play with the band, and he'd write out all the music too. So, one day, Sammy came in and he told Sunny – 'Your name is Le Sony'r Ra.' It just came out of his mouth: 'That's your name – Le Sony'r Ra.' So Sun Ra realised

something was telling him that this was his spiritual name. And from that moment, he used Le Sony'r Ra."

iii. The curse of the red fez
Were the group at Birdland already wearing the kind of stage costumes the Arkestra wear now? When did that start?
"We started off, in the trio, just wearing ordinary clothes. But when we got to eight pieces, in Birdland, we started wearing fezes, red Egyptian fezes. We began the gig on a Monday night, I think, and I noticed that while we were playing there were some men standing in the doorway; three guys, staring at us. The next night the club owner said, 'You all can keep the gig, but you gotta take off those hats!' These guys, whoever they were, had evidently told him they didn't like us wearing the fezes. So the only way we could keep the gig was to wear different hats.

"We were wearing standard band uniforms then. We moved on to work at a place called the Wander Inn, and that's when we started wearing the robes and different-type hats. Our manager went out and bought an opera company's clothes, a lot of fantastic robes and stuff. That's when we started using little miniature spaceships, too – we'd put 'em out and let 'em run around the stage."

iv. Sun Ra on the moon
Was Sun Ra already interested in outer space, ancient Egypt – the whole astro-black mythology idea?
"Oh yeah, yeah! Egypt, philosophy, Hebrew, his knowledge of the Bible! He was always far in advance, always researching. That's all we used to do in Chicago – study, study, study. Reading different types of books, different philosophies: Voltaire, Ouspensky, Russian philosophy, Madam Blavatsky, the fourth dimension – all that stuff. Sun Ra's not the type of person to take things at face value, he has to study and make sure his research is valid.

"He used to print papers to take out to the community, to try to drive away some of the ignorance they had about the Bible and things; to open their minds to different interpretations. He was into that already. And the Muslims got a lot from him – the Black Muslims, Elijah Muhammad, they were based in Chicago at that time. Every time they would see Sun Ra, they'd crowd around and try to find out what he was

about— They would sort of antagonise him, in order to get him to talk (*chuckles*). They got a lot from him, like a Negro being a dead body."
What was that?
"Sun Ra used to print that in his papers. He said that 'c' and 'g' were interchangeable, and that Negro actually came from the word necropolis or necromancy – you just substitute the 'g' for the 'c'. He said it was a psychological trap that black men had been put into, that being called Negro meant being the equivalent of a dead body, or a person who couldn't function. That was the kind of wisdom he was spreading around Chicago.

"Plus he was always telling people to be ready for the Space Age, computers— He said there were gonna be electronic instruments that you could blow. People said, you'll electrocute yourself! You can't do that, you'll blow up! They used to laugh at him and call him 'On the moon man'. But what he told 'em, that we were gonna walk on the moon and that, all of it happened. He was very advanced in his predictions and his research, even when I first met him."

III

Loquacious about Sun Ra, Gilmore shows less interest in discussing the other musicians he's worked with. Concerning his time with the Messengers, he mentions only that while he was away Pharoah Sanders took his chair in the Arkestra! It seems Gilmore and Art Blakey did not always see eye to eye; and while the drummer has denied rumours that he fired the tenorman, he did remark to *Cadence*'s Bob Rusch: "(John'd) be telling me about his fans on Mars or Jupiter, but I said it's the fans on this planet we're concerned with."

Most of Gilmore's handful of sideman-appearances are extremely hard to find now, but four in particular are worth seeking out. Two are quartet dates – *Turns* (1964), *Bliss* (1967); two are with groups led by his Chicago schoolfriend Andrew Hill – *Andrew* (1965) and *Compulsion* (1967). *Turns* features Gilmore with Paul Bley, Gary Peacock and Paul Motian, and followed some live gigs the group had played in New York's Greenwich Village. (At that time, says Gilmore, the Arkestra were going through a bad patch financially, so Sun Ra was happy for him to find a little work elsewhere.) The live gigs sound *very* interesting: "Albert Ayler used to come up and sit in with us sometimes. Sunny Murray, too. We had a nice time." The concerts were billed as the Gary Peacock Quartet, but *Turns* is definitely Bley's record and comprises a set of tunes by his then-wife Carla. The group spin them out into freeform, but without losing sight of the structures: it's a fascinating balancing act, with Gilmore's dark-toned daubs and streamers of sound among the high points of a consistently intriguing date. The session, made for Savoy, was not released at the time: 11 years later Bley released five of the tracks on his own IAI label (on the lp *Turning Point*); and, finally, in 1987, Savoy issued the complete session (on lp and cd) for the first time – a mere 23 years late!

Bliss, available under Chick Corea's name on the Muse label, had first appeared as *Turkish Woman At The Baths* and was originally the date of drummer Pete LaRoca, who provides all the tunes. Less quirkily original than Bley's, indebted to Coltrane's modal mode and with a touch of Eastern mystery, they still make for attractive listening, with Gilmore's big sound surprisingly supple in his jinking runs. *Andrew*, a quintet lp with Gilmore sharing front line duties with vibist Bobby Hutcherson and Hill himself, also offers some fine examples of the saxophonist's sinuous phrasing. But *Compulsion* (like *Andrew*, on Blue Note) is arguably the more adventurous record, with Gilmore and trumpeter Freddie Hubbard wailing over a dense, whirling bedrock of African percussion: it also provides a rare glimpse of Gilmore's bass clarinet, forceful and keening on 'Premonition'.

Mention of Hill brings a smile to Gilmore's face.

"They're very good records, yeah! I enjoyed 'em. Andrew and I have been good friends all our lives. We went to school together – I've gotta picture of him and me, we're about six years old, wearing our short pants—," he lets out his deep-throated chuckle. "When I went into the Air Force, Andrew was playing mellophone – and he wasn't too *good* a mellophone player, I might add. But when I came out of the Air Force, this cat's playing all kind of piano. I said, what! I was so surprised. Boy, he was playing *excellent* piano."

When I remark that Gilmore has played with some of the most original post-war pianist/composers – Ra, Bley, Hill, Elmo Hope – he nods genially.

"Well, a pianist is always looking for somebody who can interpret his music like he wants it to be heard. And if he hears a cat who can do this, he's gonna hire him. I've always been good at interpreting what a writer wants from his music; that's been one of my main fortés. I can get the sound they want, the feeling they want. They recognise this, and that's why they use me."

Talk of Gilmore's tenor style prompts a question about early influences – and a surprising answer.

"Stan Getz."

Huh? The guy whose personal signature in the Arkestra has long been an ecstatic, high-register scream maintained at fever-pitch for minutes on end was influenced by the mainstream's Mr Smooth!

"At the time I started tenor I was in an all-white band, remember, and all they used to play was Stan Getz. So he was a big influence on me until I heard Sonny Stitt and Sonny Rollins – then they wiped that influence out! But Lester Young and Dexter Gordon were two of my very first favourites, so it wasn't too much of a surprise that Stan Getz influenced me. Till I had a furlough and I went back to Chicago to see my friend George Eskridge. He was a fantastic guitarist and teacher. He played me Sonny Stitt and Bud Powell on 'Bud's Bubble'. I said, whoa, this is what's happening? Then I heard Sonny Rollins on 'Paper Moon' – I went, oh *shucks*, I'm behind (*laughs*)! I said, man, I got some catching up to do."

IV

i. Tomorrow's news today

I guess this is the ultimate question. You've stayed with Sun Ra for almost 40 years – why? What's the big attraction?

"The wisdom, the learning. Being with Sun Ra is like being with— oh, tomorrow's newspaper headlines. Because he knows what's gonna happen before it happens. He'll predict things off the top of his head that you'll see come true three, six months later, a year later. You say, damn, the cat told us! This is constant with him, predicting things that are gonna happen. There's never a dull moment. Plus the music is *hard*. He's got some stuff it's so hard it's unbelievable, it'll blow your mind! Makes you wish you had another hand or more fingers, so you could play it."

ii. A fast-moving vibration

Is any of this on record?

"Very little, because it's difficult to get a whole bunch of guys to play it. Maybe one or two cats can play it, me and Marshall (Allen) maybe— I don't know if we have 'Cosmic Co-ordinator' on record, but that's a very hard number. It changes tempo – 7/4, 3/4, 5/4 – quick, no preparation, you know. Sun Ra can write that kind of stuff, but there wouldn't be any point for him to be continually writing stuff that cats can't play. So he has to write mostly according to the people he has and their ability."

Couldn't he make more small-group records with guys who can play the harder music?

"We did do a few, but Sun Ra doesn't like small groups too much. He can't use the harmonies and structures he likes when he's limited to four or five pieces. And why should he be limited when he's got all this knowledge about chords, structure, harmony?

"He's *un*limited in his ability to write challenging music – stuff that you maybe have to spend hours or weeks on just to get to it, to really play it. So you never get bored – the challenge is always there. And you get used to that, to being around a fast-moving vibration! You know if you go anywhere else, it's a slow-down – you'll start going backwards (*chuckles*). I'm not gonna run across anybody who's moving as fast as Sun Ra, so I just stay where I am."

June 1990

EVAN PARKER
Speaking Of The Essence

Imagine: beard, spectacles, tenor or soprano sax. Already many music-lovers will be thinking 'Evan Parker'. Master instrumentalist, advocate for free improvisation, creator of a singular solo music, Evan Parker is one of the modern era's most extraordinary and original voices.

The ex-botany student-cum-jazz fanatic who came to London in the mid-60s and made his mark playing with SME, Parker's biography is too well-known to need further rehearsal here. In the last 25 years he has played in a variety of contexts, from the Charlie Watts big band to the Michael Nyman ensemble, but his first allegiance has always been to free improvisation. That vocation he has pursued particularly in two long-standing trios – with Barry Guy and Paul Lytton; with Alex von Schlippenbach and Paul Lovens – and, since 1974, in the context of solo saxophone performance, becoming one of the finest of all solo improvisers.

I met with Evan on 18/1/91 and our three-hour conversation produced enough material for three or four articles. In this instance, I've chosen to highlight some of the more abstract areas we touched upon. Free improvising may be the most ancient of musical practices but it remains the hardest to describe; Evan, I think, comes as close as anyone has to naming the unnameable. In part one he talks about how and why he improvises and about his music's links (or not) to the jazz tradition, to politics, to metaphysics; in part two he recalls a few of the musicians who inspired him to play; in part three he traces the evolution and practice of his remarkable solo music, that sensuous, finespun soprano sound-flow with which, helped by circular breathing techniques, he is able to create "the illusion of polyphony".

For the sake of clarity, I've occasionally included the questions and/or quotations which sparked Evan's replies, but most of what follows is uninterrupted Parker. The snake, who appears in such titles as *The Snake Decides* and 'The Snake As A Road Sign', is, says Evan, a very personal and resonant symbol for him. Perhaps these are the aphorisms of the snake, as told by a master charmer.

1. Stepping Through The Wall: Group Improvisation

"I still use the word 'jazz'. For me I'm playing jazz." Evan Parker, 1973.

•

"What's important to me is that my work is seen in a particular context, coming out of a particular tradition. I don't really care what people call it, but I would want it to be clear that I was inspired to play by listening to certain people who continue to be talked about mainly in jazz contexts. People like John Coltrane, Eric Dolphy, Cecil Taylor – these were the people who played music that excited me to the point where I took music seriously myself. That continues to be the case. That's where what I'm doing has to make most sense, if it makes any sense at all."

•

"If you relate to that tradition, I think there comes a point where you either have a personal voice or you don't. If you don't, you continue to be talked about as somebody who sounds like someone else. And if you do, you start being talked about as somebody who other people sound like!"

•

"It's been fantastic for me to play in the last couple of years with Cecil Taylor because he was one of my inspirations when I was still learning to play. Especially in group improvisation terms. That original trio with Jimmy Lyons and Sunny Murray was, for me, more interesting than the trio of Albert Ayler, Gary Peacock and Sunny Murray, though that was also fantastic. It was to do with the looseness of it all, the *openness* of the interaction; that it wasn't based on a pre-given grid, either of a harmonic scheme or a metric scheme. OK, there may have been some compositional, motivic elements at work, but the improvisations are very organic – based on listening and interaction."

•

"The continuity with the jazz tradition is there— it is in the energy and intensity both of the feelings and of the way they are expressed." Ian Carr on Evan Parker, 1973.[1]

•

"Of course the music expresses something, but I'm not sure whether it's as simple as expressing how you feel and that being the intention or the aim. My aim is often to make myself feel better by playing (*laughs*)."

•

There seems to be a curious paradox in group improvisation, because to play with artists such as Cecil Taylor or Peter Brötzmann you presumably have to have a very strong musical personality; yet there's the ideal that this is leaderless music too, that it goes beyond egos.

"The closest I got to playing without ego, in that sense, was probably in the Spontaneous Music Ensemble with John Stevens. There was a lot of talk about, how can we get to the real *group* free music? And it did seem to be about the fragmentation of any one particular contribution, so you could see it had parallels with Webern and *Klangfarbenmelodie* – that notion of the total group statement not being derivable from superimposed linearities but from pointillistic, atomised contributions. So, if you analyse any one of the players, you don't hear a coherent line; it's only by putting the whole thing together that you hear a coherent group music.

"Nobody was really telling anybody else what to do, but there was something being aimed at. That old record, *Karyobin*, gives you some idea of what I'm talking about, but probably the best examples never got recorded. They were played for audiences of five or six people."

•

"In the summer of 67 or 68 Peter Kowald came over, and he was playing very much out of a Gary Peacock obsession, the type of playing Gary Peacock did with Albert Ayler. So we played with him, and through him made connections with the German scene, with Peter Brötzmann and later Alex von Schlippenbach. Their whole approach was a much more robust, energy-based thing, not to do with delicacy or detailed listening, but to do with a kind of spirit-raising, a shamanistic intensity. And I had to find a way of surviving in the heat of that atmosphere.

"I dunno— at some point, I think I was aware of a schizophrenic quality: having to play *this* way with German musicians, *that* way with Dutch musicians, *another* way when I got home. But after a while those contexts became more interchangeable and more people were involved in the interactions, so all kinds of hybrid musics came out, all kinds of combinations of styles. Because in the end it's about recognisable individual styles.

"Maybe it's to do with having a certain confidence about what you stand for, which you can take into any situation. So it becomes much more your responsibility to *bring* something to the situation, rather than waiting to make an appropriate response. If everybody does that, then nothing happens because nobody makes the first move."

•

"When the music's really going you switch from left-brain activity to right-brain activity – and once you've made that switch the left brain can think about more or less anything it wants. The laundry, anything."
Evan Parker, 1985.

•

"The speeds of decision-making that are involved in group improvisation go beyond analytical thought, in the same way that playing Chopin must go beyond analytical thought. There are— larger patterns involved, which have to be grasped as patterns – of speed, of intensity."

•

So are you aware of what you're playing as you're playing it?
"You're very aware. You're absolutely *in* it. Of course there's a certain amount of anticipation and tactical considerations which help to make the bigger shape. But on a detail for detail level, it's not done by adding one thing to another, it's done by— instantaneous is the wrong word because you've done it *before* you've even thought about it. You can only listen to it—"
As it happens?
"—after it's happened (*laughs*). But you've done it before you've thought of it."

•

"There's an analogy with the spokes on a revolving wheel. Everything's in motion, the rim of the wheel is supported by the spokes, but when the whole thing is turning you don't see the spokes any more. If the thing didn't have that speed of rotation, it would make sense to count the spokes and think about them one at a time. But the whole point is to get the thing revolving and the spokes are only there to enable the rim of the wheel to turn. There's some kind of equivalent to that in the music. You could, you can, after the event, slow the thing down and look at how all the pieces fit together. But the whole point is that those pieces fit together in that way in order to generate the speed of movement which *is* the music."

•

"The music is not what you hear by analysis, it's what is there in the real time of the performance."

•

If not by analysis, how do you carry forward your music?
"A lot of the idea of going forward will be to do with what sound like very technical considerations. Because that's the only way you can think about the possibilities. It's as though the emotional content can only be conveyed by a technical vehicle which evolves. So the emotional message remains the same, but in order for it to retain its meaning and its freshness, the technical content of the music has to change."

•

"What happened with 'The Woe' was, we couldn't ignore the war, we were in *the war, therefore to stay in the music we had to let the war in the music and the music became war."* Steve Lacy, 1982.

•

"The way Steve integrates improvisation and composition is anyway rather different from the kind of so-called free improvising that the groups I organise do. So a situation like that wouldn't arise. I don't think it would because the music is— it's a medium of transcendence. It's not about mundane matters. Whatever you want to call that other dimension – mystical, spiritual, cosmic – it's the recognition that music has a chance to generate emotions, feelings, thoughts, which are *meta*physical: not worldly, other-wordly. That's the attraction.

"And maybe, in the worst case, escapism, in the sense of running away from reality, comes into it. I prefer to think— I think it was Brahms who said to somebody that they have religion, but we have something better – speaking of music."

•

"Which is not to say that I don't have political thoughts. But I don't think about them as having the same kind of possibilities for me as the music does. Because it's a separate world. Or, in the words of John Stevens, 'another little life'. It's as though you step through a wall, in the way that a character does in one of Doris Lessing's novels. The heroine steps through the wall and starts to live her life on the other side, which is in a slightly different time and place. That's how it is. Music, freely improvised group music especially, is a way of stepping through the wall to another place where things are, in some ways, more straightforward."

•

"If you look at music as a continuum between two polar extremes, then at one extreme is a music that is totally predictable because you know everything in it from start to finish; at the other extreme there is music that is so surprising you have trouble understanding it as *music* – say an indeterminate piece by John Cage.

"I guess I like to be closer to the pole that is about the unknown and the unfamiliar. But at the same time I want to feel that it's *about* something, that it has meaning. So the aim is not to 'let sounds be sounds', or however Cage put it, but to acknowledge the fact that producing the sounds means something to you, being in control of the sounds means something to you, interacting with the other players means something to you. And have the outcome, the musical outcome, be at least an expression of these things."

•

You mentioned meaning. Can I ask about the snake motif in your recent titles – The Snake Decides, *'The Snake As A Road Sign'?*
"I played at the Serpentine Gallery and I started to think about the shape of the lake as seen from the air, the curving lines of the music— Then the snake is a symbol of many things, especially of treachery and— untrapability, poisonousness, danger. Plus the other things – the snake charmer, hypnotism, self-renewal. There was a compound set of resonances, some of it very personal, very private imagery. And, for me, a sense that somewhere behind this, there's a meaning. A syncronicity. So that was it – certain things came together. I thought, well, this is a kind of personal symbol for you."

•

"I wanted it to be clear that this snake continues. The title 'The Snake As A Road Sign' is an aphorism from Canetti's *The Human Province*, which has extracts from diaries, notebooks, in the period from the 40s to the 60s, I think. The idea of a snake as a road sign is very funny to me. Funny and illuminating. You're going to ask, in what way? In a poetic way. Yes, that's a cop-out (*laughs*)!"

2. The Uncontainable Spirit: Heroes

"Improvisation doesn't lay very well with people who are trying to keep the music in a nightclub kind of context, or in an entertainment context, because familiarity is an important ingredient of the jazz that gets played in those contexts. So even if the solos are out, at least there's a theme to come back to at the end. You can see the pattern of development that the music has taken has been about the business and cultural administrative forces that would like the music to remain in an entertainment medium and the forces that would like it to be a totally creative artform."

Hasn't there always been that same war? You could say establishment forces tried to stop Charlie Parker, John Coltrane. Isn't it the same cycle again?

"Well, that's a big series of questions. I'd rather talk about things I know than speculate on what happened to Charlie Parker. One can only guess that there were tremendous pressures to make him conform, and to package him and make him more acceptable. But his spirit was uncontainable in that sense. You could put him with strings, put him with any kind of unlikely thing, make him play Cole Porter— suggest any of the ways of presenting Charlie Parker to the world, and *still* he manages to come through as, well, as a genius, a unique creative process.

"Same thing with Coltrane. OK, there are those stories about what happened after he ruined his mouthpiece. The thing that he told Frank Kofsky, that he ruined his mouthpiece soon after the Village Vanguard sessions.[2] And there is a brief period after that in the recordings where things are— safer – the *Ballads* album, the date with Johnny Hartman, those kind of easier projects compared to the intensity of the live performances. But they've still got that unique— *presence* – of Coltrane, the individual. Whatever he does is interesting, is touched by that *spirit."*

•

"But it's clear that there are forces maybe speaking in the left ear, and other forces speaking in the right ear. And musicians always have to juggle with, oh, survival, their ego—you know, difficult problems. And if somebody says, look, play this way and you'll be rich and famous, then obviously you might think, well, yeah, I'll try it – I'll try rich and famous for a bit (*laughs*)."
Have you ever been tempted?
"Nobody's ever— I must admit that nobody's ever whispered in my ear (*laughs*). I don't think they have."

•

You've mentioned Dolphy and Coltrane as influences?
"Eric Dolphy's influence— People say, well, I haven't got a clue what he's talking about there, but a lot of the solo work is about having the instrument sound in different registers. OK, Dolphy did that by moving rapidly from upper to lower register, by having figures that were clearly spread across three different registers, whereas my approach is to maybe have all those things sound at the same time. So it's technically very different. But the idea of the potential of the saxophone as a constant presence, to have all the range present in the listener's sensibility at the same time, you could say that is a structural influence.

"In the case of Coltrane – my choice of instrument, of everything, was determined by that influence. It's hard to pick any one thing. Maybe *the* most important was his ability to move on from what he'd already done to something else. In the most exceptional way. I can't think of any other player who was prepared to *abandon* so much of what they were about in order to move to the next thing. And it speaks of the *essence* of improvisation – that ability to abandon what you know in favour of moving towards the unknown territory.

"But it has to be counterbalanced with his legendary practice sessions. You know, somebody goes out in the morning and leaves him working on a phrase, and when they come back at night he's still working on a variation of the same phrase. So there was a lot of hard work, too. I'm thinking of the étude-like quality of some of the improvisations, especially in the 'Giant Steps', 'Countdown' type of chord sequences. And the elements that are in common between takes of, say, 'Giant Steps', which are recorded months apart, suggest that a lot of it was worked out. It wasn't simply a fresh response each time to a set of changes and chord symbols, but was actually a well-rehearsed compendium of phrase-long solutions to particular harmonic cadence problems. That's completely different from the approach of the later music, the modal and polymodal approach that he adopted later on. Very few people have that ability to solve the same problems in three or four different ways."

•

"I would like to retain a proper sense of humility in trying to explain what Coltrane's music— what audible kind of effect Coltrane's music has on my music. It's very different. I hope you can turn this into English. I'm a bit lost for words."

•

You've also cited Paul Desmond as an influence.
"Yes, for the lyricism, the lyrical development of the improvisation. Especially that floating kind of sound. Which, when you investigate it, it's pretty clear some of that was to do with Lee Konitz. The whole Desmond/Brubeck thing can't be considered in isolation from Konitz/Tristano. Subsequent influences have had much more weight on me; I started to think about other things and never really went into the way that Paul Desmond's music is put together. But I still find his records very moving, even though I suppose it's the last thing anybody would think of saying – that I'm a lyrical player in that tradition."

•

"It's great to be able to talk about my heroes."

3. Taking The Note For A Walk: Solo Saxophone

"The evolution is there, but only when you look backwards. It wasn't that in 1974 I decided it would be a good thing if I could evolve a solo music that would sound like the way it does now."
But having come a certain way?
"You still don't know where it's going (*laughs*). It's much easier to talk about where you've come from than to say where you're going next."

•

"When I first started to think about trying to be original – which is as awkward a proposition as it sounds, but at some point you have to decide: what am I trying to do? what am I trying to sound like? – I thought the space, the *niche*, that I could look for was somewhere between Albert Ayler, Pharoah Sanders, with some of the floating quality of the way John Tchicai played. I thought I could achieve— not exactly a synthesis, but I could work my way through the gaps that were left between what those people were doing.

"In the case of Ayler it was to do with his access to the overtone, the altissimo register, overtone control of the instrument. In the case of Pharoah, it was to do with his articulation, certain kinds of double-tonguing, triple-tonguing. And in Tchicai's case, to do with his way of floating over already a non-metric pulse, on those New York Art Quartet records. To spell it out, it sounds very mechanical but I was actually *emotionally* moved to want to be in that space. It wasn't just a calculation, I felt an *impulse*."

•

"Once you start to have an idea about what your sound is, then that becomes your reference, your context. Because you approach something in a consistent way, you do generate something recognisable, something you can start to think of as *your* sound, *your* approach. And then everything starts to be channelled into that: like, would this be an appropriate way to go? So, yes, you *are* pushed in a particular direction by decisions that you've already made, which then become internalised and inseparable from your viewpoint. Even though you're nominally free to go anywhere, you become *protective* of a certain notion of yourself, what you are, your sound."

•

"It was evolved simply to fill the space that was all mine. Suddenly it's all yours!"

•

"My evolution in solo playing has been to exploit technical possibilities and acoustic possibilities unique to the solo situation. When you have all the spaces to fill, you can listen more closely to the specific resonances in the room, to the specific interaction with the acoustic, to the overtone components in the sound – the harmonic components in any one note become much more audible. The temptation to fragment individual tones into their harmonic components becomes very attractive because you can hear yourself that much more closely; you can hear the *detail* of what's happening in any one sound."

•

You never record your solo music on the tenor saxophone?
"In concert I usually play at least one piece on the tenor, because I don't want to— let myself be scared away from trying to play the tenor solo. But until recently I haven't been happy enough with any of it to make a record. Part of that is to do with the problem of recording the tenor solo – the microphone positions tend to be difficult, even when you're using ambient microphone techniques. The way the lower frequencies of the tenor saxophone excite the room – excite technically, I don't mean emotionally (*laughs*) – the way the air molecules in the room are moved by the lower frequencies generated by the tenor saxophone is much harder to control, in the way that I want to control it."

•

"Which is not to say there aren't seven minutes here or six minutes there that I've been happy with. But I have not yet got to the point where I felt like I could make a whole record of solo tenor music. I could make a mixed record of some pieces soprano, some pieces tenor – I have thought about that – but in the end, for me, the coherence of a record depends on it not being assembled from too many fragmentary components

"I'm not terribly happy about the idea of putting a record together from several different sessions. It's important for me that records be representative of what was actually happening that day. The art of solving some of the contradictions between improvisation and recording is to make sure that I prepare well for the record and have a reason for recording; and the mental focus that the preparation brings about should then avoid the necessity of 'choosing the good bits'.

"OK, there are various technical reasons why not every note is usable. You have to do some tests for levels, and maybe a tape runs out at the wrong moment. But I would like to think that the improviser's discipline in the studio is to play and be recorded, and have that be the record. Because every step you take away from that is moving away from the act of improvisation towards the act of composition."

•

"I'm currently interested in approaching the challenge of reconciling free improvisation with studio recording in a slightly different way. I'd like to work with shorter— forms is the wrong word— shorter duration for pieces. You can work with short durations and it's almost as though you're trying to improvise a larger form through the use of short pieces. That's what I want to get to. To edit as you go, to construct the pieces according to the bigger form you seem to be evolving."

•

How integral to your music is the circular breathing?
"You remember I spoke before about certain processes being necessary to get the wheel up to speed. The circular breathing and the continuous sound is a very useful way of getting the solo engine up to speed for me.

Because once the sound has been ringing in the room, in your ears, in the instrument for a certain period of time, it's as though it aids the shift to the right brain."

•

"There's a kind of danger in being too clear, even too clear with myself, about how these things work. Because if I try to make an analytical method out of how to become non-analytical, then I'm involving myself in some strange contradictions (*laughs*)."

•

"My solo playing at the moment is about overtones and polyrhythms and using certain kinds of polyrhythmic fingering patterns in order to generate the illusion of polyphony. It's a bit like juggling— You have to do the easier tricks first: get into the rhythm and suddenly your body is able to do things which you couldn't do cold.

"The best bits of my solo playing, for me, I can't explain to myself. Certainly I wouldn't know how to go straight to them cold. The circular breathing is a way of starting the engine, but at a certain speed all kinds of things happen which I'm not consciously controlling. They just come out. It's as though the instrument comes alive and starts to have a voice of its own. The reed. It's especially strange to discover that the reed can do things— it can apparently be playing high, medium and low in distinct patterns, all at the same time."

•

Could this become a trap? That you'll be known as 'the guy who does the circular breathing'?
"I'm aware of the problem, the potential problem, there. There is a pointillistic way of improvising. How a soloist would do that, I guess, is to improvise in relation to the background noise. I think some of Anthony Braxton's solo recordings use silence fantastically – the *Series F* pieces are amazing! Pointillistic is not exactly the word for it— but it's very much the opposite of filling the whole space. I would like to feel

that I'm able to give that kind of improvisation as well; and there is a kind of weakness in playing to your strengths or in knowing the things you can do well and always going to those places. But, qualifying that, as I've said, what I'm interested in right now is working with overtones and polyrhythms. That's the way things have come down."

•

"Finished, it's finished, nearly finished, it must be nearly finished." Opening lines to *Endgame* by Samuel Beckett, EP's favourite author.

•

"There are two ways of ending for me. One is where the thing unravels. If you think about the music as the pattern in a carpet – you know how the fringe of a carpet is made out of the warp, you can see the component threads? Sometimes it's interesting for me to let the thing unravel, so the pattern is gradually pulled apart and you're left with only the threads, the strands.

"Or another way – and, again, this is me observing what tends to happen rather than me describing a plan of action – is the complexities reach such a pitch that they cancel one another out and you get a blur of— almost like white noise. Not white noise but an impenetrable kind of thickness. The whole thing *locks*. It's a gridlock. Everything locks solid and – it stops!"

•

"There's also the question about the lack of perceivable form for the listener. I think any music that deals with, that involves, circular breathing and repetition is, in a certain sense, playing with time perception, whether you like it or not. It's not so clear to me whether there's an objective reaction – it seems that some people can find every minute seems like an hour and for others an hour just seems to pass in a minute."

•

"There's no form in the sense of having a bigger architectural notion that the playing then provides the details for. There do tend to be shapes. It tends to move from simple to complex, and then it either ends on maximum complexity – which is a sort of wedge form; or it comes back— very often there are elements of *da capo*, back to the top. So there are rough analogues of normal theme and variations; there are formal qualities there. But again, it's not always a conscious plan. It's only in the course of playing that I know which form will be used. Or which form will be the most accurate way of describing what happened."

•

"It's playing with an absolutely minimal form, namely linearity. The piece starts at A and goes to B. It's not necessarily a straight line, but – a line. And that's a very natural thing for a monophonic instrument."

•

"The thing I always come back to is Paul Klee's description of drawing – taking a line for a walk. I think of solo saxophone as taking a note for a walk. And we'll see afterwards where we went rather than me leading you round a path I know well."

•

"Every time I start it's the same place and every time I start it's somewhere different. It depends on how you want to look at that place. The same as when you get up in the morning, it's a new day, but it's also got a hell of a lot in common with the day before (*laughs*). It's a question of how you want to incorporate the cyclic, repetitive elements into the Heraclitian flux, the river you can never step in twice. Both things are true and both things are absolutely inadequate descriptions of reality."

•

"Even the small reality of the music itself— When you start to talk about the bigger reality of the music, the culture, the world, the cosmos, everything else, history, cosmology, the small story of the music in that context becomes a very strange little nothing.

"But maybe because it is nothing and has no sense of real power, strangely enough it has a kind of— it seems to be able to allude to some bigger picture. But never in a way that could help anybody decide what to do when they get up tomorrow (*laughs*). Not really. Not even me. Unless it's to practise."

But perhaps it can help you decide to *get up tomorrow* (laughs)?

"Ah! Yes. Perhaps."

January 1991

1. Ian Carr, *Music Outside* (London: Latimer, 1973).
2. Frank Kofsky, *Black Nationalism And The Revolution In Music* (New York: Pathfinder Press, 1970).

Discographical Update

The interviews in this book cover a ten-year period. During that time the advent of the cd has caused the virtual annihilation of the lp. Many cds too, both of new and reissued music, have appeared only to vanish again in the blink of an eye as items go in and out of catalogue with bewildering rapidity. And, of course, most of the artists discussed in the book have continued to record and issue new music that is certainly no less worthy of attention than their previous work. So, rather than attempt a complete discography of the discs mentioned in the text, I've chosen instead to list a *selected* discography that comprises currently-available cds (as of 12/93) and includes releases that post-date the interviews.

Steve Lacy has recorded prolifically in the last decade and several of his early albums have been reissued on cd, including *The Straight Horn Of Steve Lacy* (Candid), *Evidence* (OJC) and *The Forest And The Zoo* (ESP). For his work with Cecil Taylor, see below. His first session of Monk tunes, *Reflections* (with Mal Waldron), has been reissued on OJC, while among more recent examples of his passion for Monk are the sextet disc *We See* (hat ART) and two solo tributes, *Only Monk* and *More Monk* (both Soul Note). Lacy also appears on the excellent salute to Herbie Nichols, *Change Of Season* (Soul Note). His *Songs* collaboration with Brion Gysin has been reissued by hat ART, but I think a more succesful marriage of music and words is the later *Futurities* (hat ART, two discs), which features a nine-piece Lacy ensemble working with poems by Robert Creeley. Other fine Lacy group cds include *Momentum* (Novus), *The Gleam* (Silkheart) and *Morning Joy* (hat ART). A 1992 solo version of 'The Way', here called 'Tao', appears on the solo hat

ART cd *Remains*; the same label plans to reissue the 1979 group version on cd in 1994.

Cecil Taylor too has released a constant stream of new recordings in the 80s and 90s, the most notable being the 11-disc set *Cecil Taylor In Berlin '88* (FMP), which features him in various line-ups with some of Europe's leading improvisers (the discs are also available separately). Other recent sets well worth a listen are the big-band *Winged Serpent (Sliding Quadrant)* and the solo *For Olim* (both Soul Note), plus the small-group *Live In Bologna* and Taylor's sound-poetry cd *Chinampas* (both Leo). His hat ART recordings have been reissued on cd (*One Too Many Salty Swift and Not Goodbye* and *Garden* are probably the most essential), as have the 1976 Enja solo *Air Above Mountains – Buildings Within* and several of his earlier works, including *The World Of Cecil Taylor* (Candid), *Conquistador* and *Jazz Advance* (with Steve Lacy) (both Blue Note).

Mal Waldron's *The Quest* is an OJC cd. Some of his Enja records have been on cd, but none are currently available; conversely, his various hat ART duos with Steve Lacy are scheduled for reissue but have yet to appear. One date with Lacy that is in catalogue is the duo *Sempre Amore* (Soul Note), a charming collection of Ellington tunes. Also available are his ECM disc *Free At Last* and two enjoyable duos with alto saxophonist Marion Brown, *Songs Of Love And Regret* and *Much More* (both Freelance).

Many of **Abdullah Ibrahim**'s Enja recordings are also unavailable on cd; two you can get are the solo *African Sketchbook* and the duo *Echoes From Africa* (with Johnny Dyani). *Water From An Ancient Well*, by Ibrahim's group Ekaya, is on Blackhawk.

There are no recordings of **Chris McGregor**'s solo piano music on cd and no discs as yet by Brotherhood Of Breath, though Ogun hopes to release a Brotherhood cd in the near future. Chris died in May 1990, just a few weeks before his fellow-Blue Note Dudu Pukwana. Louis Moholo, now the sole surviving Blue Note, co-organised the tribute album, *Spirits Rejoice* (Ogun), which boasts a big band of leading UK improvisers (under the name of the Dedication Orchestra) playing pieces by McGregor and his colleagues.

My favourite **Billie Holiday** recordings are the dates she made for Commodore in 1939 and 1944. These are temporarily out of catalogue.

I'd also recommend nearly all of her Columbia sessions.

The only 'early' **Mike Westbrook** on cd is 1975's *Citadel/Room 315* (Novus). *Bright As Fire: The Westbrook Blake* has been reissued by Impetus and *The Cortege* is now a two-disc Enja release. Both *Westbrook-Rossini* and *On Duke's Birthday* have been reissued by hat ART.

There is still no sign of **Norma Winstone**'s early music on cd and only a few signs of her more recent work. There is just one Azimuth disc available – *Azimuth '85* (ECM). Her plans for a duo cd with John Taylor have yet to materialise (a privately-produced tape has appeared and may be available from specialist shops or at her concerts). But she did record the beautiful *Somewhere Called Home* (ECM), with Taylor and Tony Coe, which for me is the best British jazz vocal release for many years.

Max Roach's *We Insist! Freedom Now Suite* seems to go in and out of print on different labels in different countries with alarming alacrity. His *Percussion Bitter Sweet* (GRP/Impulse!) is certainly available, as are his duos with Cecil Taylor – *Historic Concerts* (Soul Note); and Anthony Braxton – *Birth And Rebirth* (Black Saint), *One In Two – Two In One* (hat ART). A good cross-section of his current activities can be heard on the two-cd *To The Max!* (Enja), which has tracks by his post-bop quartet, his work with string quartet and voices, two pieces with his percussion ensemble M'Boom and a couple of scintillating solo drum tracks.

Betty Carter's 1969 live sets, *Finally* and *Round Midnight*, are now on cd on Roulette and the 1979 *The Audience With Betty Carter* is on Verve. I'd recommend these over her more recent studio discs.

The *Tapscott Sessions* reached seven volumes on lp and a volume eight has appeared on cd (Nimbus). A 1989 live concert featuring **Horace Tapscott** with Cecil McBee, Andrew Cyrille and guest John Carter has been issued by hat ART – *The Dark Tree* (two discs, available separately). And, at last, *The Giant Is Awakened* has been reissued, as part of the *West Coast Hot* cd (Novus). Sonny Criss' *Sonny's Dream*, featuring Tapscott compositions and arrangements, is on OJC.

The **Guest Stars** have long since disbanded. None of their music made it on to cd. But guitarist Deirdre Cartwright now leads her own group (with Alison Rayner on bass) and hopes to record in the future.

Marilyn Crispell's music continues to go from strength to strength. *Gaia* is now on cd and later trio recordings include *Live In*

Zurich and *The Kitchen Concert* (all Leo). Solo discs include *For Coltrane* (Leo), *Labyrinths* (Victo) and the magical *Live In San Francisco* (Music & Arts). She has also released several duo recordings – with Anthony Braxton (Music & Arts), Georg Gräwe (Leo), Gerry Hemingway (Knitting Factory) and Irene Schweizer (FMP) – plus two outstanding ensemble cds, the explosive *Circles* (Victo) and the austerely romantic *Santuerio* (Leo). Marilyn is now the proud owner of two chairs.

All of **Dave Holland**'s ECM recordings as leader, save *Emerald Tears*, are on cd. The early *Conference Of The Birds* and the 1990 quartet *Extensions* are good places to start. *Phase-Space*, a 1991 duo with alto saxophonist Steve Coleman, is on DIW. Holland's work with Anthony Braxton can be sampled on the latter's superb *Dortmund (Quartet) 1976* and *Town Hall (Trio & Quintet) 1972* cds (hat ART); his recordings with Sam Rivers include two discs of improvised duos on IAI and Rivers' quartet disc *Waves* (Tomato).

Sunny Murray's ESP debut has been reissued on cd, as have his Freedom and ESP sessions with Albert Ayler (*Vibrations*, *Spiritual Unity*, *Spirits Rejoice*, *Bells* and *New York Eye And Ear Control*). None of his work with Cecil Taylor is currently on cd. Though Murray has recorded little in recent years, there is a fine duo set with pianist Alex von Schlippenbach, *Smoke*, on FMP and he can be heard playing with reedsman David Murray on the latter's *A Sanctuary Within* (Black Saint).

The **Jimmy Giuffre** 3's *Thesis* and *Fusion* lps have been reissued by ECM as the two-cd set *1961* (but *Free Fall* has still to reappear). The Giuffre/Bley/Swallow trio reformed in 1989 and recorded *Life Of A Trio: Saturday* and *Life Of A Trio: Sunday* for Owl, followed by 1992's lovely *Fly Away Little Bird*. Hat ART has also unearthed two 1961 concerts by the JG3 – *Flight, Bremen 1961* and *Emphasis, Stuttgart 1961*. *Dragonfly*, *Quasar* and *Liquid Dancer*, by Giuffre's electric quintet, are on Soul Note.

Kenny Wheeler's ECM dates, with the exception of *Around 6*, are on cd. *Flutter By, Butterfly* is a Soul Note cd. Releases that post-date our interview include the quintet *The Widow In The Window* plus the two-disc *Music For Large And Small Ensembles*, which has several tracks by the big band referred to in the article (both ECM). *Kayak* (Ah Um) is a nice set by an 11-piece ensemble. A few examples of Wheeler's work with Anthony Braxton are on the latter's *Live* cd (Novus), while his work with Dave Holland's quintet is on the *Jumpin' In*, *Seeds Of Time* and *The Razor's Edge* cds (all ECM).

Leo Smith's *Procession Of The Great Ancestry* is still on Chief and is still magnificent. More good news is that ECM has issued a new Smith solo recording, *Kulture Jazz*, which proved one of my favourite releases of 1993. ECM also plans to reissue *Divine Love* in 1994, and Black Saint has already put *Go In Numbers* on cd.

Sun Ra left the planet in May 1993, bringing to a close one of the most brilliant and extraordinary artistic endeavours of the 20th century. We are fortunate that at least a portion of his legacy is in the hands of the diligent and conscientious Evidence label, which has adhered to the very highest standards in terms of sound-quality, documentation and packaging. To date Evidence has reissued 19 of his lps (mostly from the 50s/mid-60s era) on 14 cds, including such essential titles as *Jazz In Silhouette*, *Cosmic Tones For Mental Therapy*, *Interstellar Low Ways*, *The Magic City* and *Fate In A Pleasant Mood*. A 15th Evidence cd, *Soundtrack To Space Is The Place*, contains previously unreleased music from 1972. Sun Ra's three mid-60s ESP discs have also been reissued on cd, as have the later *Sunrise In Different Dimensions* (hat ART) and *Strange Celestial Road* (Rounder). Best of the recent releases are probably *Live at Pit-Inn* (DIW) and the beautiful, valedictory *Mayan Temples* (Black Saint). Blast First issued a limited-edition cd of extracts from the Mean Fiddler concert: called *Live In London 1990*, it's well worth seeking out, though the sound quality is less than perfect. Two videos, *Space Is The Place* and *A Joyful Noise* (both from Rhapsody Films), are also highly recommended.

John Gilmore can be heard on most of the above Ra discs. Of his other work, *Turns* is, I think, no longer available, but the shorter IAI set *Turning Point* is on cd. Unfortunately, Blue Note has not yet reissued the excellent Andrew Hill lps on which Gilmore plays.

The **Evan Parker** Trio, with Barry Guy and Paul Lytton, has a live cd, *Atlanta*, on Impetus, while Parker's work with the Alex von Schlippenbach trio is on *Elfen Bagatellen* and *Physics* (both FMP). Parker's classic solo records on Incus are out of catalogue, but *Conic Sections* (Ah Um) is a fine example of his 'pure' solo music. Contrary to expectations, the later *Process And Reality* (FMP) finds him experimenting with multitracking – and, as promised, shorter durations. I'd also recommend his duos with Walter Prati on *Hall Of Mirrors* (MM & T), Steve Lacy on *Chirps* (FMP) and Anthony Braxton on *Duo (London) 1993* (Leo). The early Spontaneous Music Ensemble classic, *Karyobin*, has just been reissued by Chronoscope Records; the line-up is Parker, Derek Bailey, Dave Holland, John Stevens and Kenny Wheeler.

Finally, for readers looking to extend their listening into other areas of modern (ie post-1955) creative music, below are 30 favourite cds not already mentioned above. I've restricted myself to a single entry per artist, with the exception of Anthony Braxton, who gets four because I think he is a genius. Happy listening!

Albert Ayler *In Greenwich Village* (Impulse!)
Ran Blake *Suffield Gothic* (Soul Note)
Paul Bley *Solo Piano* (Steeplechase)
Anthony Braxton *Creative Orchestra Music 1976* (Novus)
    Quartet (Coventry) 1985 (Leo)
    2 Compositions (Ensemble) 1989/1991 (hat ART)
    Willisau (Quartet) 1991 (hat ART)
John Carter *Castles Of Ghana* (Gramavision)
Ornette Coleman *The Shape Of Jazz To Come* (Atlantic)
John Coltrane *My Favourite Things* (Atlantic)
Paul Desmond *Easy Living* (Novus)
Bill Dixon *Son Of Sisyphus* (Soul Note)
Eric Dolphy *Out To Lunch* (Blue Note)
Duke Ellington *The Far East Suite* (Novus)
Dennis Gonzalez *Stefan* (Silkheart)
Julius Hemphill *Live At The Cafe Society* (Music & Arts)
Andrew Hill *Shades* (Soul Note)
Franz Koglmann *L'Heure Bleue* (hat ART)
George Lewis *Homage To Charles Parker* (Black Saint)
Booker Little *Out Front* (Candid)
Warne Marsh *Two Days In The Life Of—* (Storyville)
Joe McPhee *Oleo & A Future Retrospective* (hat ART)
Charles Mingus *Presents Charles Mingus* (Candid)
Roscoe Mitchell *L-R-G/The Maze/S II Examples* (Chief)

Thelonious Monk *Live In Stockholm 1961* (Dragon)
David Murray *Ming's Samba* (Portrait)
Herbie Nichols *The Art Of Herbie Nichols* (Blue Note)
Hal Russell *The Finnish/Swiss Tour* (ECM)
Lucky Thompson *Tricrotism* (Impulse!)
Henry Threadgill *You Know The Number* (Novus)

I think it's clear from reading these lists that fans of contemporary jazz owe a great debt to the handful of European labels that have championed the music over the last two decades. (It's arguable that label owners such as Giovanni Bonandrini and Werner X. Uehlinger have done at least as much to ensure the continuation of 'the jazz tradition' as Wynton Marsalis has!) If you have trouble finding their releases in the shops, they can be ordered from their respective UK distributors:
Black Saint, hat ART and Soul Note from Harmonia Mundi, 19-21 Nile Street, London N1 7LR;
ECM and Enja from New Note, Electron House, Cray Avenue, St Mary Cray, Orpington, Kent BR5 3RP;
FMP from Cadillac, 61 Collier Street, London N1;
Leo cds can be ordered directly from Leo Records, The Cottage, 6 Anerley Hill, London SE19 2AA.

Index

Abdullah, Ahmed *147*
Abrams, Muhal Richard *97*
Adams, Pepper *37*
Ade, Sunny *111*
Aebi, Irene *19*
Ali, Luqman *151*
Ali, Rashied *31, 122*
Allen, Marshall *147, 150, 151, 152, 163*
Altschul, Barry *115, 116*
Ammons, Albert *22*
Ammons, Gene *37*
Archer, Robyn *64*
Armstrong, Louis *21, 88*
Art Ensemble Of Chicago, The *13, 147*
Aston, Laurence *70*
Ayler, Albert *15, 27, 60, 119, 120, 121, 123-124, 142, 147, 151, 161, 166, 167, 174, 184, 186*
Azimuth *77, 78, 79, 80, 140, 183*

Bach, J.S. *48*
Bailey, Derek *114, 137, 186*
Baraka, Imamu Amiri (aka LeRoi Jones) *36*
Barriteau, Carl *136*
Barry, Robert *157-158*
Bartók, Béla *117*
Basie, Count *157*
Beatles, The *13, 22, 92*
Bechet, Sidney *18*
Beckett, Harry *61*
Beckett, Samuel *178*
Benjamin, Bea *47*
Bennett, Richard Rodney *137*
Berger, Karl *106*
Biscoe, Chris *67, 71*
Blackwell, Ed *84*
Blake, Ran *98, 186*
Blake, William *68, 71-72, 73, 74, 76, 108, 109, 183*

Blakey, Art *21, 84, 86, 121, 160*
Blank, Roger *145*
Blavatsky, Madam H.P. *159*
Bley, Carla *130, 161*
Bley, Paul *129-131, 132, 156, 160, 161, 184, 186*
Blue Notes, The *57, 59-60, 61, 182*
Bluiett, Hamiet *49*
Blythe, Arthur *96, 97*
Bonandrini, Giovanni *187*
Botha, P.W. *52*
Bradford, Bobby *96*
Bradshaw, Tiny *46*
Brahms, Johannes *169*
Brand, Dollar – see Ibrahim, Abdullah
Braque, Georges *18, 21*
Braxton, Anthony *14, 86, 87, 88, 105, 106, 107, 111, 113, 114, 115, 116, 117, 127, 138-139, 147, 177, 183, 184, 185, 186*
Brecker, Michael *139*
Brookmeyer, Bob *129, 133*
Brotherhood Of Breath, The *57-58, 61, 62, 182*
Brötzmann, Peter *166, 167*
Brown, Clifford *13, 42, 84*
Brown, Everett, Jr. *97*
Brown, James *32*
Brown, Marion *147, 182*
Brown, Ray *129*
Brubeck, Dave *173*
Burning Spear *85*
Bynner, Witter *19*

Cage, John *119, 170*
Calloway, Cab *67*
Canetti, Elias *171*
Capone, Al *71*
Carne, Marcel *36*
Carner, Gary *146*

INDEX

Carr, Ian 69, 76, 76fn, 135, 166, 180fn
Carroll, Lewis 32
Carter, Betty 14, 89-95, 183
Carter, John 96, 183, 186
Cartwright, Deirdre 101, 183
Catlett, Sid 121
Chancey, Vincent 147
Charig, Marc 61
Charles, Ray 91, 93
Cherry, Don 19, 47, 49, 60, 123
Chopin, Frédéric 31, 48, 167
Circle 115, 117
Clarke, Kenny 83-84
Clements, Vassar 114
Coe, Tony 137, 183
Coleman, Ornette 13, 19, 26, 47, 96, 117, 130, 186
Coleman, Steve 115, 184
Coltrane, John 13, 18, 26, 35, 36, 37, 39, 41, 42, 47, 50, 56, 71, 78, 84, 105, 106, 112, 121-122, 147, 156, 161, 165, 171-173, 184, 186
Company 113
Compton, Denis 52
Cooper, Lindsay 73
Corea, Chick 115, 161
Creeley, Robert 181
Crispell, Marilyn 105-111, 183-184
Criss, Sonny 96, 97, 183
Cupido, Josefina 99-103
Cyrille, Andrew 27, 28, 122, 183

D'Silva, Amancio 78
Da Mango, Linda 100, 101
Daisical, Laka 99-104
Dankworth, John 135, 136
Davis, Anthony 110, 142
Davis, Charles 147
Davis, Eddie 'Lockjaw' 157
Davis, Miles 78, 84, 86, 90, 91, 114-115, 116, 123, 143
Davis, Richard 147, 158
Debussy, Claude 129
Dedication Orchestra, The 182
Deep River Boys, The 46
Delius, Frederick 79
Delmar, Elaine 115
Desmond, Paul 173, 186
Dickinson, Debbie 101
Disney, Walt 145
Dixon, Bill 186
Dolphy, Eric 13, 27, 35, 36, 39-40, 41, 42, 84, 96, 122, 165, 172, 186
Doyle, Julia 101

Droulers, Pierre 21
DuBois, W.E.B. 124
Dyani, Johnny 19, 57, 182
Dyer, Sammy 158

Edwards, Teddy 96
Eicher, Manfred 79
Ekaya 182
El'Zabar, Kahil 143
Eldridge, Roy 143
Ellery, Sue 101
Ellington, Duke 26, 31, 47, 48, 50, 51, 52, 55-56, 58, 61, 62, 67, 68, 69, 74, 75-76, 95, 97, 140, 147, 182, 183, 186
Ellison, Ralph 14, 25
Eskridge, George 162
Eubanks, Robin 147
Evans, Gil 19
Evans, Nick 61
Evans, Richard 158

Fab Five Freddie 87
Farmer, Art 37
Favors, Malachi 148
Fawkes, Wally 114
Fayenz, Franco 146
Feza, Mongezi 57, 60, 138
Fitzgerald, Ella 35
Flamingos, The 91
Fortune, Sonny 49
Fournier, Vernel 158
Fox, Roy 136
Freeman, Von 147
Frisell, Bill 133
Fugs, The 109
Funkadelic 147

Garbarek, Jan 139
Garner, Erroll 26
Garrick, Michael 78
Garvey, Marcus 39, 85
Gaye, Marvin 30
Getz, Stan 114, 115, 116, 162
Gibbs, Mike 137
Giddins, Gary 31
Gillespie, Dizzy 83, 86, 91, 143
Gilmore, John 14, 146, 147, 150, 151, 152, 156-163, 185
Gismonti, Egberto 77
Giuffre, Jimmy 127-134, 184
Globe Unity Orchestra, The 137, 141
Gonzalez, Dennis 186
Gordon, Dexter 96, 99, 162

Goya, Francisco *20, 73, 75*
Graves, Milford *122*
Gräwe, Georg *184*
Gray, Wardell *96*
Green, Benny *94*
Greer, Sonny *26*
Griffin, Johnny *145*
Grimes, Henry *27*
Grimes, Kitty *79, 81fn*
Guest Stars, The *99-104, 183*
Guy, Barry *164, 185*
Gysin, Brion *18, 21, 181*

Hall, Jim *128-129, 133*
Hammond, Doug *115-116*
Hampton, Gladys *91*
Hampton, Lionel *69, 91, 92, 97*
Harper, Winard *94*
Harriott, Joe *78, 137*
Harris, Craig *147*
Hartman, Johnny *171*
Hawes, Hampton *96*
Hawkins, Coleman *37, 84*
Hawkins, Erskine *46*
Hayes, Tubby *136*
Haynes, Roy *125*
Hearndon, Jim *158*
Hemingway, Gerry *184*
Hemphill, Julius *186*
Henderson, Fletcher *146, 147, 152*
Henderson, Joe *138*
Hendrix, Jimi *22, 114*
Hentoff, Nat *26, 28, 31, 34fn*
Herman, Woody *128*
Hicks, John *94*
Higgins, Billy *147*
Hill, Andrew *13, 97, 156, 160, 161, 185, 186*
Hill, Tyrone *150*
Hines, Earl *13*
Hines, Gregory *121*
Hodges, Johnny *26, 86*
Holiday, Billie *13, 35, 36, 37-39, 64-66, 90, 106, 182-183*
Holland, Dave *112-118, 139, 140, 184, 185, 186*
Hooker, John Lee *91*
Hope, Elmo *156, 161*
Hubbard, Freddie *85, 156, 161*
Hutcherson, Bobby *161*

Ibrahim, Abdullah (aka Dollar Brand) *13, 14, 44-56, 59, 60, 182*

Institutional Church Of God In Christ Choir, The *87*

Jackson, Ronald Shannon *27*
Jamal, Ahmad *158*
James, Doug *108*
James, George G.R. *149-150*
Jarrett, Keith *139*
Jarvis, Clifford *147*
Jazz Epistles, The *46*
Jazz Messengers, The *84, 156, 160*
Johnson, James P. *127*
Johnson, Oliver *19*
Jones, Elvin *84, 121-122*
Jones, LeRoi – see Baraka, Imamu Amiri
Jordan, Clifford *156*
Jordan, Duke *90*
Jordan, Louis *45*

Kaplan, E. Ann *66fn*
King, Rev. Dr. Martin Luther, Jr. *83, 87, 88, 143*
Klee, Paul *179*
Knight, Gladys, & The Pips *91*
Kofsky, Frank *171, 180fn*
Koglmann, Franz *186*
Konitz, Lee *129, 173*
Korner, Alexis *136*
Kowald, Peter *167*

La Violette, Dr. Wesley *128, 130*
Lacy, Steve *13, 14, 17-22, 27, 29, 41-42, 169, 181-182, 186*
Lake, Oliver *106*
Lancaster, Byard *119*
Land, Harold *84, 96*
LaRoca, Pete *156, 161*
Lawrence, D.H. *67, 68*
Lemer, Pepi *78*
Lessing, Doris *169*
Lewis, George *134, 186*
Lewis, Meade Lux *22*
Lincoln, Abbey *33, 36, 39, 48, 84, 85, 87*
Lindwall, Ray *44*
Little, Booker *36, 39, 84, 137, 138, 143, 186*
London, Julie *64*
Lorca, Federico García *73*
Lovens, Paul *164*
Lowe, Frank *147*
Lundy, Curtis *94*
Lyons, Jimmy *28, 165*
Lytton, Paul *164, 185*

INDEX

M'Boom 86, 183
Macero, Teo 131
Makeba, Miriam 59
Malfatti, Radu 61
Manne, Shelly 128
Mariano, Charlie 106
Marsalis, Wynton 187
Marsh, Warne 186
Masekela, Hugh 46, 59
Matthews, Stanley 44
Max, Willie 46
McBee, Cecil 183
McGregor, Chris 57-63, 114, 137, 182
McLean, Jackie 37
McPhee, Joe 186
Meyer, John 137
MFSB 150
Miller, Harry 61
Miller, Keith 44
Mingus, Charles 35, 37, 40, 42, 68, 84, 117, 186
Minton, Phil 67, 70, 71, 73, 80
Miracles, The 91
Mitchell, Adrian 71
Mitchell, Red 129
Mitchell, Roscoe 106, 186
MJQ (Modern Jazz Quartet) 129
Moeketsi, Kippie 46, 59
Moholo, Louis 19, 57, 182
Monk, Thelonious 13, 17-18, 19, 21, 26, 42, 48, 50, 52, 83, 98, 106, 107, 120, 147, 181, 187
Moody, James 121
Moreland, Mantan 92
Morton, Jelly Roll 22, 67, 145
Moses 148, 149
Motian, Paul 160
Muhammad, Elijah 159
Murray, David 96, 119, 120, 124, 184, 187
Murray, Sunny 14, 27, 47, 84, 119-126, 161, 165, 166, 184
Mussorgsky, Modeste 132

Naughton, Bobby 143
Neidlinger, Buell 26, 27, 31, 34
New York Art Quartet, The 174
Nichols, Herbie 120, 181, 187
Nicols, Maggie 78, 80
Nyman, Michael 164

Oliveros, Pauline 110
Orchestra USA 129
Ore, John 147

Orioles, The 91
Ouspensky, Peter 159
Oxley, Tony 137

Parker, Charlie 37, 47, 83, 84, 86, 87, 88, 90-91, 94, 112, 114, 121, 171
Parker, Evan 14, 61, 137, 139, 164-180, 185-186
Patrick, Pat 157, 158
Peacock, Gary 123, 160, 161, 166, 167
Pena, Ralph 128-129
Pepper, Art 13
Philip, Jim 78
Phillipe, Jeanne 27
Phillips, Barre 114
Picasso, Pablo 20, 114
Porter, Cole 95, 171
Potter, Tommy 90
Potts, Steve 19
Powell, Bud 26, 83, 87, 162
Powell, Richie 84
Prati, Walter 186
Presley, Elvis 92
Priester, Julian 147, 158
Pukwana, Dudu 57, 60, 182
Purnell, Nick 136

Quebec, Ike 37, 99

Rava, Enrico 49
Ray, Johnny 114
Ray, Michael 151
Rayner, Alison 101, 183
Reece, Dizzy 156
Riley, Ben 48, 53
Rimbaud, Arthur 73
Rivers, Sam 27, 53, 113, 114, 116, 184
Roach, Max 14, 36, 39, 40, 48, 53, 82-88, 90, 121, 183
Rogers, Shorty 128
Rollins, Sonny 84, 138, 162
Rossini, Gioacchino 68, 183
Rouse, Charlie 37
Rusch, Bob 160
Russell, Hal 187

Saba, Isio 24, 25, 32, 34
Sanders, Ed 109
Sanders, Pharoah 147, 160, 174
Savoy Sultans, The 37
Schlippenbach, Alex von 137, 164, 167, 184, 185
Schuller, Gunther 129

191

Schweizer, Irene *184*
Scott, Noel *152*
Scott, Ronnie *60, 115*
Shah, Tarik *94*
Shakespeare, William *76*
Shepp, Archie *13, 27, 94-95*
Shoemaker, Bill *142, 143*
Shorter, Wayne *156*
Silver, Horace *21, 26*
Sisterhood Of Spit, The *63*
Skidmore, Alan *137*
SME – see Spontaneous Music Ensemble
Smith, Bessie *86, 88, 90, 146*
Smith, Clara *146*
Smith, Leo *106, 115, 142-143, 185*
Smith, Ruthie *101*
Smith, Willie 'The Lion' *31*
Solid Gold Cadillac *69*
Soulyard *102*
Spaulding, James *147*
Spellman, A.B. *27, 32, 34fn*
Spontaneous Music Ensemble (SME) *78, 137, 164, 166, 186*
Stevens, John *137, 166, 169, 186*
Stitt, Sonny *129, 162*
Stockhausen, Karlheinz *147, 152*
Stravinsky, Igor *22, 73*
Streamline Brothers, The *46*
Sun Ra *13, 14, 61, 144-155, 156, 158-163, 185*
Surman, John *61, 69, 78, 137*
Swallow, Steve *129, 131, 184*
Symphony Sid *37*

Talking Heads *111*
Tambo, Oliver *51*
Tapscott, Horace *96-98, 183*
Tatum, Art *18, 97*
Taylor, Cecil *13, 14, 18-19, 21, 22, 23-34, 47, 60, 86, 87, 98, 106-107, 111, 119, 120-122, 123, 125, 130, 131, 165, 166, 181, 182, 183, 184*
Taylor, John *77, 78, 79, 80, 140, 183*
Tchicai, John *174*
Teitelbaum, Richard *29*
Tell, William *68*
Temptations, The *91*
Thatcher, Margaret *52, 71, 72*
Thompson, Lucky *187*
Threadgill, Henry *187*
Tippett, Keith *78*
Tippetts, Julie *78*
Todd, Phil *73*

Towner, Ralph *79*
Tristano, Lennie *173*
Tuxedo Slickers, The *46*
Tympany Five, The *45*
Tyner, McCoy *121, 156*
Tyson, June *151*

Uehlinger, Werner X. *187*
Ullman, Michael *91, 95fn*
United Jazz + Rock Ensemble, The *140*
Untouchable Factor, The *119*

Varèse, Edgard *119, 120*
Voltaire *159*

Wakeman, Alan *71*
Walcott, Colin *114*
Waldron, Mal *13, 14, 35-43, 66, 181, 182*
Walker, Alice *64*
Walker, David *143*
Walker, T-Bone *91*
Waller, Fats *26, 58*
Ward, Carlos *49, 52*
Warnock, Peter *79*
Washington, Kenny *94*
Waters, Ethel *146*
Waters, Muddy *91*
Watts, Charlie *164*
Weather Report *132*
Webern, Anton *166*
Webster, Ben *37*
Wells, Dicky *157*
Wells, H.G. *23*
Westbrook, Kate *67, 68, 70, 72, 74, 75*
Westbrook, Mike *67-76, 78, 137, 183*
Wheeler, Kenny *77, 78, 79, 114, 115, 117, 135-141, 184-185, 186*
White, Nick *53, 57*
Williams, Martin *131*
Williams, Tony *122, 123*
Wilmer, Val *31, 34fn, 35*
Wilson, Gerald *96, 97*
Winstone, Norma *14, 77-81, 140, 183*
Wonder, Stevie *22*
Workman, Reggie *108, 110, 111*

X, Malcolm *83*

Young, Lester *13, 37, 128, 162*

Zeserson, Katy *53-55*
Zorn, John *133-134*